OTHER BOOKS BY EDWARD KANZE

The World of John Burroughs

Notes from New Zealand:
A Book of Travel and Natural History

Wild Life

Wild Life

The Remarkable Lives
of Ordinary Animals

Edward Kanze

Illustrated by Jennifer Harper

Crown Publishers, Inc.
New York

For my parents

Published by Crown Publishers, Inc., 201 East 50th Street, New York,
New York 10022. Member of the Crown Publishing Group.

CROWN is a trademark of Crown Publishers, Inc.
Random House, Inc., New York, Toronto, London, Sydney, Auckland

Manufactured in the United States of America

Library of Congress Cataloging-in-Publication Data
Kanze, Edward.
Wild life : the remarkable lives of ordinary animals
/ by Edward Kanze ; illustrations by Jennifer Harper.—1st ed.
Essays originally appeared in various newspapers published in
Connecticut and New York by Acorn Press.
1. Zoology—North America.   2. Animal behavior—North America.
I. Title.   II. Title: Wildlife.
QL151.K36   1995
591.97—dc20   95-2500
CIP

Design by Jennifer Harper

ISBN 0-517-70169-3
10 9 8 7 6 5 4 3 2 1
First Edition

Acknowledgments

All of the essays in this book appeared originally, in abbreviated and otherwise different form, in the seven newspapers published in Connecticut and New York by the Acorn Press. At the press I owe thanks to many, particularly the publisher, Thomas Nash, and my editor, a fine nature writer in his own right, Jack Sanders. For their support over the years, and for their indulgence of my often eccentric ideas, I am grateful.

Max Gartenberg, my stalwart agent in New York, helped develop the idea for this book, and Debbie Kanze, my wife, assisted in selecting the material that was polished and recast for inclusion. To Max and Debbie, and to the fellow naturalists who contributed ideas, information, companionship, and encouragement during the years in which these essays were written, I wish to express deep thanks.

At Crown, Brandt Aymar and Carole Berglie brought their considerable talents to bear on pruning and shaping the manuscript of this book into its final form. I am grateful for their good work.

Finally, I would like to thank Jennifer Harper, whose drawings bring beauty to these pages.

Contents

Part Two: Fur and Wide

Part Three: In Cold Blood

Part Four: Odds and Ends (Mostly Odds)

Preface

Powderpuff-size birds that migrate to and from Brazil without airline tickets, vultures that cool themselves by urinating on their own legs and repel enemies by vomiting on them, beavers that stroll blithely into suburban living rooms, and American toads awash in sperm during round-the-clock orgies—these are some of the animals that populate this book. For the most part, this volume explores the lives of creatures that are common and widespread—lucky and adaptable species that still thrive, despite the state of the biosphere. It may be no coincidence that these animals exhibit some of the most peculiar behaviors ever observed in wildlife, suggesting perhaps that in difficult times, eccentricity can have great practical value.

In range, the chapters embrace animals that inhabit the North American continent from Newfoundland to the Everglades, and from Point Barrow, Alaska, to Mexico City. All the beasts described are American natives, with the exception of the Norway rat and the house sparrow, which by virtue of their universal presence and convincing abundance, might as well be.

The book is divided into four sections. The first, American Birds, introduces such peculiar creatures as the black skimmer (*aka* the sea dog), a shorebird with a terrible case of underbite, and the hummingbird, perhaps the most disagreeably tempered animal in all of birddom. Elsewhere in this section the reader will find owls, crows, bluebirds, wild turkeys, mockingbirds, warblers, and a big woodpecker that remodels a suburban house.

The second section, Fur and Wide, considers some of our continent's most distinctive mammals. Included are the admirable porcupine, a beast with many strong points, and the masked shrew, which despite its kinship to the blue whale is little bigger than a bumblebee. Rounding out the menagerie are mammoths, mastodons, bobcats, beaver, coyotes, flying squirrels, weasels, opossums, whitetail deer, pronghorn, whistle pigs (woodchucks), and the bizarre, reptilelike armadillo.

The book's third division, In Cold Blood, examines an array of intriguing reptiles, amphibians, and invertebrates. Here the reader will find Charles Darwin snooping in his garden for earthworms, read about the author's near miss with a very large rattlesnake, and learn how snakes evolved from lizardlike ancestors ("The Evolution of Snakes, or A Farewell to Arms"). Hognose snakes, copperheads, frogs, toads, salamanders, beetles, butterflies, ant lions, spiders, and horseshoe crabs round out the set.

The concluding section, Odds and Ends (Mostly Odds), contains five of the author's most offbeat and whimsical forays into natural history. He presumes to include them here because, during years of writing nature essays and teaching people about wildlife, he has found that it is his outlandish writing and comments that readers most appreciate and best remember—just as people retain knowledge of extraordinary animals, the porcupines and platypi of the world, far better than they hold on to facts about the conformists, the sparrows and the mice.

PART ONE

American
Birds

1

The Warblers:
Heroes of Flight

melia Earhart opened the throttle of her 550-horsepower Wasp motor and roared down the airstrip. Her plane, loaded beyond capacity with 500 gallons of fuel and weighing over three tons, responded. Earhart eased the little craft off the improvised runway and took aim for a bank of low clouds. Night was falling in the late afternoon of January 11, 1935.

Earhart climbed to six thousand feet. There would be no turning back. If she touched down alive, the aviatrix would have completed a journey neither man nor woman had made before her: a solo aerial crossing of the eastern Pacific.

At high altitude the skies were clear. Ahead and above, Earhart saw thousands of twinkling stars; below loomed a dark, deadly void, the Pacific. She spotted a ship nine hundred miles from Honolulu and blinked her landing lights in greeting.

Every half-hour Earhart broadcast her position. In mid-crossing she spoke to her husband with the aid of an innovative new instrument called the radio-telephone.

The loneliness was intense. To dull its edge and to keep awake, Earhart nibbled on a hard-boiled egg and sipped hot chocolate from a thermos. The plane's motor roared reassuringly.

Eighteen hours after take-off, Earhart landed in Oakland an instant hero. Photographers pounced for pictures. Reporters elbowed close to hear her words of triumph. For several days, newspapers, newsreels, and radio broadcasts around the world celebrated her achievement. Earhart had challenged the Pacific and won.

One autumn morning, looking out a kitchen or bedroom window, you may notice a wren-size bird gleaning insects from the twigs of a tree. If you are a birdwatcher, you will recognize the apparition as a warbler, one of a migratory, chiefly insectivorous group of songbirds that raise their young in local woods and fields or, in the case of certain species which winter in the tropics and nest in the far north, pass through your town in spring and autumn.

This particular bird is softly streaked, has faint white bars on its wings, and is colored a pale olive. These features identify it as a blackpoll warbler.

When the blackpoll, a night-flying migrant, dropped from the sky and landed in your shade tree, no camera crews or journalists were there to record the event. Nor will any be on hand to record its departure from your neighborhood in a night or two. Yet by the time the bird entered your consciousness, this determined flying machine, weighing less than an ounce and traveling under its own steam, may have bettered Earhart's flight by more than double. Its journey, quite possibly, began in an Alaskan spruce forest six thousand miles away. And the blackpoll has not reached its destination. The most heroic part of its journey still lies ahead.

After a day of feasting on insects, the blackpoll will spring from its perch, beat its tiny wings, and fly from your tree. Night is falling. The bird soon reaches the Atlantic Coast and heads out over the sea. Up, up, and up it flies, defying the pull of gravity. Eventually it will reach a cruising altitude of about 6,500 feet.

The most dangerous part of the long solo flight to the blackpoll's wintering range is now under way. Through the next few days and nights, the tiny bird, fueled only by reserves of body fat, pumps its wings without rest. Brazil is unthinkably distant.

Jumbo jets roar by, carrying people reading magazines, devouring meals, watching movies, and flushing toilets. The warbler flies. Hours become days. Steadily the blackpoll labors southward.

The bird passes over the islands of the Caribbean at 21,000 feet or thereabouts. This is more than three times Earhart's peak altitude over the Pacific. Far below, the ocean swirls, cold and inhospitable.

Untold numbers of blackpolls fall to death in the sea; scientists and fishermen occasionally extract them from the bellies of ocean-going fish. A few tumble exhausted onto the decks of passing ships. And many blackpolls, perhaps thousands, are lost in violent storms.

At long last, a green coast looms ahead. Brazil. The blackpoll descends. Minutes later it clasps a branch, its first perch in many days. No cameras flash, no banquet awaits. For the famished blackpoll it is business as usual. Insects must be sought, captured, and consumed. In Brazil it is spring.

What Earhart accomplished with a three-ton airplane, five hundred gallons of fuel, thirty-five gallons of oil, two altimeters, three clocks, three compasses, weather forecasts, and detailed charts, the warbler surpassed with wit, muscle, and resolve. Physical endurance aside, one cannot but wonder how the blackpoll found its way.

Research findings suggest that migrating birds, including the blackpoll, depend on a variety of cues in seeking their destinations. Among these may be landmarks, the stars, the position of the sun, and the magnetism of the earth itself.

Still, we really know very little about how the warbler found Brazil, or how hundreds of other species of migratory birds find their way between summer and winter homes.

Like the last chapter in the life of Amelia Earhart, who vanished without a trace during another Pacific flight, the last word on the blackpoll has yet to be written.

2
Owls by Day,
Owls by Night

Owls, with their upright postures and soulful eyes, seem to share our pretensions to superiority. For all appearances, they are little flying men in feathered suits—sprites or fairies that live quietly among us.

Like sprites and fairies, owls are hard to see. We share our cities, suburbs, and countryside with the birds yet glimpse them rarely because they inhabit a universe parallel to, but separate from, our own. They sleep not far from our sleeping places, hunt near the supermarkets where we shop for groceries, and stuff dismembered animals into the mouths of their nestlings within half-hearted hooting distance of our cribs and high chairs. Yet owls and humans do not generally cross paths. They function in different niches of time. In owl time, humans flock to electric lights like oversized moths, or sleep. In human time, owls roost in trees, sleeping, or trying to. The upshot is that few of us, save for die-hard birdwatchers and the most observant insomniacs, actually get to see these airborne homunculi alive, perched or on the wing.

Of course, not having seen an owl is nothing to be ashamed of. In their time, the feathered tigers of the night are all but invisible to us, and they are masters of concealment in ours. Put an owl in a tree, step back a few paces, and without budging an inch the little Houdini vanishes.

This is how they do it. Owls are cryptically colored. That is, their plumage provides a camouflage matched exactly to the natural colors and shapes of their environment. The first thing an owl does to make itself disappear is *nothing*. It just sits there. Sticks, bark, sunlight, and shadows do the rest.

Owls often heighten the effectiveness of their camouflage by stretching to their vertical utmost. If you ever have a chance to observe a roosting owl first-hand, you will be amazed just how tall and skinny a rotund bird can become.

Normally, trees don't have fat lumpy things sitting on their limbs. They do, however, retain the truncated stubs of branches broken off in storms. By elongating, an owl transforms itself into a perfect replica of one of these stubs and disappears.

The niftiest ruse in the vanishing-act repertoire of owls is the horns-on-the-head trick. This bit of subterfuge can be employed only by owls with the requisite headgear—in my neck of the woods, the screech owl, the long-eared owl, and the great horned owl. Above their eyes, these birds have tufts of feathers that resemble (use your imagination) the horns of goats and antelope.

Scientists long thought that owl horns aided the birds in hearing. This theory was set aside after one researcher who was probably a frustrated hair stylist snipped off the tufts of several birds and found that they could hear just as well without them. Today, the most widely held theory is that the horns are instruments of camouflage—that is, they serve to break up a bird's outline as it sits in its daytime roost.

If you manage to get a look at a horned owl, it will probably be the result of scrutinizing the same area of a tree for several minutes. When you finally see the bird, looking down at you and blinking in annoyance, it will be hard to understand why you didn't see it sooner. Ah—then you note how the horns completed the masquerade. The top of the owl's head looks exactly like the irregular end of a damaged branch.

How, then, to locate owls if they're so darned hard to see? The lazy man's way—the method I prefer above all others—is to let crows do the work.

Crows despise owls. Owls probably would despise crows if, to paraphrase an exchange between Humphrey Bogart and Peter Lorre in *Casablanca*, they thought about them long enough. Certainly owls eat crows from time to time. This undoubtedly goes far toward explaining why crows (intelligent birds by any standard) feel as they do. In daylight, when a crow spies an owl, it makes a lot of noise. Other crows soon arrive and join the ruckus. Before long the branches around the owl fill with scads of crows—especially if the owl at the center of attention is a great horned.

The next time you see dozens of crows gathered in a tree, screaming in unison, stop whatever it is you are doing. (If you are driving, first pull off to the side of the road.) Go to the place where the crows are, crossing swamps and streams where necessary. Approach the tree slowly, and as you do, look long and hard among its branches.

If the crows are screaming half-heartedly, you will probably see a hawk. But if the big black birds are hurling accusations with genuine fervor, a dusky bird with broad wings and a body shaped like a beer keg may soon fly off, dragging the entire squadron of prosecutors behind it. If that's the case, you will have gotten a rare glimpse, however brief, of a real live owl.

3

The Louisiana
Waterthrush:
A Song of Spring

You, you, you—listen 'cause I'm won-der-ful-ly mus-i-cal. So says, or seems to say, the Louisiana waterthrush, announcing its annual return to North American haunts after a winter in the tropics. About the middle of April, along woodland streams, this bird drowns out its neighbors with a flood of song.

Despite its name, the Louisiana waterthrush is not a thrush. It belongs to a group of compact, insectivorous, migratory songbirds known as the wood warblers. Like a thrush, however, Monsieur Louisiana has a dark back and a white speckled breast. Unlike a thrush, he is fast moving and, in temperament, downright effervescent.

Everyone loves a happy extrovert. Every man, woman, and child would love the Louisiana waterthrush, if only the bird were easy to see. But it lives in deep woods, in lonely ravines transected by rushing streams. Only early-season fly fishermen and birdwatchers who seek the waterthrush enjoy its music and antics.

The female waterthrush is more elusive than the male. She, like he, skulks along streamsides, plucking emergent mayflies from twigs and boulders and snatching a few from the air. But whereas the male gives away his position by singing from time to time (sometimes all the time), the female bird keeps quiet, and to find her you must be persistent. Waterthrushes must be approached with stealth because, when intruders appear, birds of both sexes will flee upstream or downstream, escaping to the distant reaches of their long narrow territories.

Fortunately, hearing a Louisiana waterthrush provides a far greater thrill than seeing one. The song has a joyous quality, and it is delivered with verve and exuberance. Hal Harrison, a great authority on American songbirds, writes that the Louisiana waterthrush utters a song that "I can truthfully describe as exciting." This is strong praise from a man who states flatly, "I consider wood warblers to be mediocre songbirds at best." Listen to the waterthrush song in its proper milieu—in a woodland, in a shady ravine, near a stream running cool and fast—and you will likely be thrilled to the soul.

What is the source of magic in the waterthrush song? Such things are not easily analyzed, but the answer, I suspect, lies in the song's associations—its geographical link to quiet woods and rushing streams, and its temporal connections with the onset of shirtsleeve weather, the blooming of wildflowers, and the reappearance of leaves on the trees.

To hear a Louisiana waterthrush for yourself, you must visit a streamside. A good time to begin listening for the bird is around the tenth or eleventh of April. The performance is launched with two, three, or four (most often three) clear ringing notes. Each has a distinct downward slur. *You, you, you* is a fair approximation. Then follows a bubbling, wrenlike collection of high-pitched tones. These roll and tumble over each other like droplets of water in a rapids. Translating the second half of the song is a challenge, so swiftly do the notes spill out. To me it suggests the words *listen 'cause I'm won-der-ful-ly mus-i-cal*.

In April, rarely will you find me at my desk, hammering out essays. More often I'm out of doors, down by a stream, skulking from pool to pool like a trout fisherman. Back home, there's a sign upon my door, saying, "Gone Listening."

4

The Mockingbird: Do You Hear What I Hear?

s it just my imagination, or are the mockingbirds these days vocal to an extraordinary degree? I hear the great feathered polyglot everywhere I turn—in the tops of shade trees, in meadows, on telephone wires, along suburban streets, in bushes, on branches, showering the landscape with whistles, clucks, whines, cackles, trills, and glissandos. "Listen to the mockingbird," an old song advises. Is it possible *not to*?

An encyclopedia of bird lore in my library asserts that mimicry, in terms of the total singing of a mockingbird, accounts for a mere 10 percent. Is this possible? Certainly it cannot be so in spring and summer. Certainly it is not true at six in the morning, at eight in the evening, and (you who read these words with bloodshot eyes will agree) between midnight and sunrise, in the time generally supposed to be the dead of night. As I see and hear it, mockingbirds sing and mockingbirds imitate, loudly and tirelessly, around the twirling clock.

The more sounds you learn to differentiate in the environment, the more impressed you will become with the mockingbird's mimetic prowess. It is not unusual for a particular mockingbird to imitate the songs of thirty or more species of songbirds. Once I sat on a neighbor's lawn and listened to a mockingbird's repertoire that included the sounds of killdeer, blue jays, great crested flycatchers, tufted titmice, red-bellied woodpeckers, flickers, Carolina wrens, catbirds, and cardinals. The bird also imitated a gray treefrog and a police siren.

How exact are mockingbirds at duplicating sounds? According to John Terres's *Encyclopedia of North American Birds*, scientists with sophisticated electronic equipment have scrutinized the imitations of mockingbirds and found the counterfeit calls perfect copies of the originals. As tangible proof of the point, I submit an example close to home. At my house, no sound is more familiar than the soft but grating whine of the family dog. Ben, a basset hound, pleads insistently to be put outside, and soon after getting what he wants, commences whining to be let back in. For better or for worse, a mockingbird has mastered Ben's plaint. Now I hear the whining of a basset hound throughout the days and evenings—even when Ben is asleep. In a typical day I venture to the door several times to let Ben in, only to discover him padding up behind me. Ben himself is fooled. He lobbies to be put outside more often these days—to investigate the prospective but nonexistent playmate he hears beckoning from the yard.

Why do mockingbirds (and catbirds, brown thrashers, starlings, crows, and a host of other birds around the globe) sing the songs of other species? No one really knows. There are several theories. Imitating may help individual mockingbirds to develop their own unique calls. Or it may be a form of play, or a means of venting excess energy, or a strategy for diminishing competition with other birds by giving the impression that a territory is awash in songbirds of myriad species. Whatever the explanation, there is undoubtedly sound method behind the mockingbird's madness. Mockingbirds, to my ears, seem more numerous, and more vocal, than ever.

5

Thoreau's "Most Serene Birdship," the Bluebird

The blue of an indigo bunting is jazzier, the song of a rose-breasted grosbeak is more melodic, and the symphony delivered by the male winter wren suggests greater virtuosity. Yet none of our songbirds excites quite the same admiration as the bluebird.

Perhaps bluebirds win an edge over rival songbirds by virtue of their early arrival in spring. In local meadows and orchards, they appear in mid-February, just as the sap begins to rise in the sugar maples. Brooks roar with snowmelt, and in the meadows you can hear the first soft warbles of the bluebirds.

Bright hues are rare in the winter woods, so the bluebird flocks that wing in from the south provide welcome bursts of color. Henry David Thoreau compared the year's first bluebird to "a speck of clear blue sky seen near the end of a storm."

A hundred years ago, most Americans recognized bluebirds as surely as they knew the faces of their children and neighbors. Bluebirds were abundant because the farms that European settlers and their descendants hacked out of the continent's woods offered the sunny, open environment in which bluebirds thrive. As farms and farmers proliferated, so did the bluebird.

But more changes were in store. In the late nineteenth century, several types of birds native to Europe were brought to America and released. Among them were the skylark, the nightingale, the starling, and the house sparrow. Neither skylarks nor nightingales adapted to New World conditions, but starlings and house sparrows, which are aggressive and adaptable birds, flourished. This meant hard times for the bluebird. Starlings and house sparrows began building their nests in old woodpecker holes—sites which previously had been occupied by bluebirds—and as the populations of the European birds expanded, those of the native bluebird declined. In a few decades there were hardly any bluebirds left at all.

In the nineteenth century, few educated people would have mistaken bluebirds for blue jays, but confusion is commonplace today. Except for the matter of color, two birds could hardly be more dissimilar in appearance and behavior, but the uncertainty which prevails is easily understood. In most places bluebirds are uncommon and little seen.

Blue jays are big (larger than robins) and noisy. They have crests on their heads, long tails, white bellies, and a variety of stripes and chevrons superimposed on the faint blue of their backs. Eastern bluebirds, on the other hand, are somewhat smaller than robins, to whom they are closely related. Seen at a glance, a bluebird has much the same profile as a robin: a handsomely rounded head of moderate size, a plump belly, and a downwardly inclined tail of moderate length.

The color of the male bluebird is striking. The blue is rich in hue, appearing sky blue in bright sunlight and heavy indigo in deep shade. Thoreau suggested that the bluebird "carries the sky on his back." "In certain lights," he wrote, "nothing can be more splendid and celestial than the color of the bluebird."

The breast of a male bluebird is earthy brown, suggesting the color of a freshly plowed field. Acknowledging Thoreau's metaphor and carrying it a step further, John Burroughs wrote: "When nature made the bluebird she wished to propitiate both the sky and the earth, so she gave him the color of the one on his back and the hue of the other on his breast, and ordained that his appearance in spring should denote that the strife and war between these two elements was at an end."

Female bluebirds are similar in color to the males, although their hues are more subdued. In her own subtle way, the female is just as striking as her dashing suitor.

When the bluebird sings, its warble is soft and gentle. In music and in poetry the voice of the bluebird has come to represent peace and goodwill. As I write, a male bluebird serenades his mate just outside my window. He hopes, I suspect, to lure a female into a nesting box on an old cedar pole that holds up the north end of my clothesline. His notes of entreaty are warm and seductive; if I were a female bluebird, I'd fly to him at once.

Thoreau, an aficionado of bluebird song, found in the placid behavior and calm voice of the bluebird a model of serenity. He suggested the bird be hailed as "His Most Serene Birdship." "Princes and magistrates are often styled serene," wrote the Concord naturalist, "but what is their turbid serenity to that ethereal serenity which the bluebird embodies?"

In recent years, inspired by the writings of Thoreau, Burroughs, and others, humans have begun to help the bluebird. It has long been known that bluebirds, lacking natural woodpeckers' holes in which to raise their young, will nest in wooden boxes, and these boxes can be built and installed in ways that keep them largely free of starlings and sparrows. Today, people of goodwill are putting up such boxes from New York to California, and bluebird numbers are rising.

In the corner of the world where I have lived much of my life, two men deserve the lion's share of credit for aiding in the bluebird's return. I cite their example because it is well worth emulating.

The first of the two, Beresford Proctor, retired after a long and prosperous career as a banker. Not wanting to spend his remaining years grazing in a back pasture, he began to build bluebird houses. He used the best available materials (redwood scraps donated by a sauna manufacturer and galvanized nails he bought himself) and gave the finished products to landowners and nature sanctuaries that were interested in joining the cause. Today, more than three thousand boxes later, Proctor is ninety-three and still going strong.

The second man, Tom Meyer, is a friend of the first. He puts up most of the boxes that the first man makes, and between nestings (bluebirds in my area raise two or three broods of nestlings each season), he cleans the boxes, which helps protect the young birds from parasites. Meyer watches the boxes closely, repairs them when they're broken, and relocates them when he decides another spot will prove more hospitable to bluebirds. Several hundred bluebird boxes are under his care. His services are provided free of charge. In the warm months the work amounts to a full-time job.

Thanks to these men, and others like them, I can sit here at my writing desk happy in the knowledge that bluebirds are calling just outside my window.

6

Owls Go A-Courting

Live with me and be my love,
And we will all the pleasures prove.
That hills and valleys, dales and fields,
And all the craggy mountains yields.
—Shakespeare

On a dark night in the dead of winter, a tenor voice shatters the silence of the woods.

Hooo, hoo-hoo-hoo.

Before the last emphatic note dies away, a reply is launched. It comes in a rich disembodied basso that seems to radiate not from a single point but from every direction at once. The tone is soft, and it manages to sound both soothing and fearsome.

Hoooo, hooo-hooo, hoooo, hoooo.

The duet continues for an hour. Songbirds, recognizing the voice of doom and darkness, shiver in their nighttime roosts. Screech owls, taking no chances, glance over their shoulders as they go about their mouse hunting. Cross-country skiers shuffle across a nearby meadow and are reminded of the lateness of the hour, the long journey home. In the woods, great horned owls are courting.

Every winter, sometime in late December or early January, the courting rites of the great horned owl commence. Males and females mate for life, but they fly solo much of the year, hunting independently, sleeping in separate roosts by day, even launching attacks on each other from time to time. At Christmastime or thereabouts, a change of heart occurs. Rising hormone levels in the male and female owls revive urges suppressed for months. The birds begin to roost together, to face life's troubles side by side.

For great horned owls, troubles come not as single spies but chiefly as battalions of aggressive crows. Crows harass owls mercilessly by day, and often, in order to salvage something of a day of rest, a sleepy great horned owl must retreat deep into the forest, to a pine or spruce so dense that its branches offer sanctuary from the prying eyes of crows. After darkness falls, of course, the owls seek revenge.

As winter progresses, the bond between the male and the female great horned owls grows stronger. The male hoots often and reaches his best voice and peak of garrulity around the end of January. His call is deeper, longer, and more involved than that of the female. Her voice is higher and more *staccato*, and in comparison to his, is delivered at a faster, more *allegro* tempo.

Those who venture into the winter woods at night may hear the owls calling. Their voices sound muffled and far away, even when the owls are close. Like others of their clan, great horned owls are skilled ventriloquists.

Henry Thoreau heard an owl hooting near Walden Pond on a December evening in 1856:

> *The pond is perfectly smooth and full of light. I hear only the strokes of a lingering woodchopper at a distance, and the melodious hooting of an owl, which is as common and marked a sound as the axe or locomotive whistle. Yet where does the ubiquitous hooter sit, and who sees him? In whose wood-lot is he to be found? Few eyes have rested upon him hooting; few on him silent on his perch. . . . Yet cut away the woods never so much year after year, though the chopper has not seen him and only a grove or two is left, still his aboriginal voice is heard indefinitely far and sweet, mingled, oft, in strange harmony, with the newly invented din of trade. . . . Some of my townsmen I never see, and of a great proportion I do not hear the voices in a year, though they live within my horizon; but every week I hear the loud voice of the hooting owl. . . .*

It is not unusual to hear owls calling far off, a mile or more away. The high, warbling voices of songbirds have little carrying power because high-frequency sounds are readily absorbed by vegetation. On the other hand, the low-frequency utterances of our larger owls are long-distance travelers. (So are the foghorns of oceangoing ships and the entreaties of amorous bullfrogs. Evolution, both technological and biological, equipped ships, frogs, and owls with deep baritone voices for the same reason.) The long wavelengths of an owl's hoot weave through the forest like X rays penetrating flesh.

To date, ornithologists have written little about the mechanics of great horned owl coupling. As the nesting season approaches, the birds probably begin to make tentative advances toward each other, perhaps hooting duets from adjacent perches. The negotiations between male and female are undoubtedly delicate, for each bird is capable of inflicting serious wounds on the other. The male, who is substantially smaller than the female, is particularly at risk.

When it is hooting, a great horned owl makes a comical sight. To produce the trademark sound, the owl must cast off its stern demeanor, lean forward in an undignified manner, and thrust its tail upward. The owl looks embarrassed, and with good reason: its posture makes the wise old bird look like a common barnyard hen.

At the same time that the great horned owl hoots, it fluffs out a patch of white throat feathers. Owls have excellent night vision, but being seen by potential mates on dark nights is still a difficult business. The throat feathers, reflecting whatever moonglow and starlight are available, probably help the birds to find each other in the gloom.

And find each other the birds must if there are to be eggs and nestlings. Before coupling, the owls are likely to rub bills together and to help each other preen. Then, somewhere in the shadows, sometime in the coldest part of winter, the romance is consummated.

The owls go on hooting and duetting, at least for a time. To human ears the wild, untutored singing is simultaneously awful, wonderful, magical, mournful, and frightening. Always evocative of deep and fundamental emotions, it is the sound of pure wildness. To Thoreau, the song of the great horned owl suggested "the infinite roominess of nature." Upon hearing a great horned owl hooting on Christmas Day 1858, he wrote, "How glad I am to hear him rather than the most eloquent man of the age."

7
The Pileated Woodpecker: A Houdini in Feathers

F iguring out the proper cage in which to house an animal is usually a simple task. If the creature is large and powerful—such as a lion—then you need an enclosure big enough to make the lion comfortable and strong enough to keep it from breaking loose. If the prospective captive is tiny—like a mouse—then its cage should be of diminutive proportions. The critical thing in holding a mouse, of course, is to make sure there are no openings through which it can escape.

But how to house a crow-size bird with a jackhammer beak capable of blasting holes through wood, glass, and wallboard?

One August day, Dona and Glen Tracy, a husband and wife who run a clinic for injured birds of prey, found themselves faced with precisely this question. The Tracys were used to all sorts of animals appearing on their doorstep—fox kits and box turtles, for example, in addition to the anticipated hawks and owls—but a pileated woodpecker was something new.

The woodpecker arrived by limousine. A friend of the Tracys who runs an airport taxi service had been driving a pair of wealthy clients to Kennedy International Airport in New York City when he saw a pileated woodpecker attempt to fly across a busy road. The bird was hit broadside by a truck. It came to rest on the narrow shoulder of the road, perhaps dead, perhaps injured.

Oddly enough, the bird was fortunate. The man driving the cab was more devoted to animals than he was to the idea of reaching the airport on time. He pulled over, picked up the woodpecker, wrapped it in a sweater, and returned to the car. Luckily, the clients in the back were regular customers. They were familiar with the driver's idiosyncrasies and could tolerate the fact that he steered the rest of the way to the airport with only one arm on the wheel. (The other served as a seatbelt for the bird, which was content to rest calmly in the front seat, snug among the folds of the sweater.)

At the terminal, the driver deposited two of his three passengers. (The nonpaying customer remained aboard.) Then he headed straight for the Tracys', knowing that they, if anyone, could help the bird recover from its injuries.

During the trip the woodpecker perked up, crawled loose, sat briefly on the back of the front seat, and headed for the rear. There it found an armrest to its liking, and for the remainder of the journey, it perched there, looking out the window like a traveling poodle.

Although the Tracys limit their work to helping birds of prey, and a woodpecker is no more closely related to a hawk or an owl than a hummingbird is to an ostrich, they didn't have the heart to turn away the new arrival. The woodpecker needed urgent care, and anyhow its looks were winning. The combination of angular head (reminiscent of a pterodactyl), bright red crest, coal-black wings, dashing crimson mustache (identifying it as a male), and yellow eyes created a striking impression.

Among the bird's features, the crest, or pileus, was the most eye-catching. Examined up close, the headpiece was colored a brilliant vermilion. It seemed to radiate light as if it were aflame. (Looking at it was hypnotic, like staring into the embers of a fire.) The pileus had a stranded, groomed look, like that of pelage rather than plumage. It looked as if the bird had combed its feathers up and over its head in some sort of slick, 1950s-style coiffure.

The bird needed a name. Mrs. Tracy, impressed with the woodpecker's stout, chisellike beak, christened it "Spike" (a name which later proved apt).

Spike was in rough shape. He was suffering from shock, and one of his wings was broken. Mrs. Tracy isolated him in a dark, quiet room for twenty-four hours. At timed intervals, she tiptoed into the room to give him liquid nourishment through a tube. She and her husband had to resist the urge to admire their unusual patient at every opportunity. His good looks had won their hearts.

A day later, Mrs. Tracy took Spike to see a veterinarian. By this time the bird was feeling chipper, and in the waiting area, he pecked noisily on his carrying cage, generating much interest in the contents.

Mrs. Tracy later described Spike's behavior in the examination room as "nonchalant." He clung to her shirt, and from there watched calmly and with great apparent interest the comings and goings of the doctor and his assistants.

When it came time to be X-rayed, Spike cooperated without protest. The results confirmed Mrs. Tracy's initial diagnosis: the wing was broken. The doctor bandaged the damaged section and taped it to the bird's body. Thus immobilized, it would heal in about a month—if all went well.

If all went well. Keeping Spike housed, fed, and calm for six weeks or so until he could be released promised to be quite a job. It is when Mrs. Tracy brought Spike home that our story really begins.

Spike's eventful convalescence began in a cardboard cat carrier. Mrs. Tracy put the box in a quiet, unused guestroom where her patient was sure to get plenty of rest.

The carrier held Spike only briefly. He found his way out and promptly discovered a roll of carpet that stood vertically like the trunk of a tree near a window. Here, in a corner of the room, he perched contentedly.

The new arrangement seemed innocent enough. Spike kept to his perch, and he appeared to enjoy looking out the window.

There being no pressing reason to return him to the carrier, Dona decided to let Spike have his way.

One morning, after pulling into the driveway after an hour spent running errands, Mrs. Tracy was horrified to see the windowpane smashed and Spike hanging out through the jagged hole. He was, it appeared, dead. Apparently he had cut himself on the glass and bled to death.

But when Mrs. Tracy raced inside and looked into the room, she found Spike perched in his favorite spot on the rug, looking none the worse for the adventure. A breeze poured through the broken window. Shards of glass lay scattered across the floor.

The Tracys were afraid that if they let Spike remain in the room as before he would renew his assault on the window and eventually escape, hurt himself, or both. Worse, he might decide to excavate holes in the walls.

Overstated though it may seem, those familiar with the capabilities of woodpeckers in matters of woodworking know that the Tracys' concern was well founded. Alexander Wilson, the early American ornithologist and contemporary of John James Audubon, once confined an injured ivory-billed woodpecker, a cousin of the pileated, in a hotel room in Wilmington, South Carolina. While taking care of some business, he left the bird unattended for an hour, and upon returning, was startled by what he found. The captive, Wilson wrote, "had mounted along the side of the window, nearly as high as the ceiling, a little below which he began to break through. . . . The bed was covered with pieces of plaster, the lath was exposed for at least fifteen inches square, and a hole large enough to admit the fist, opened to the weather boards; so that, in less than an hour he would certainly have succeeded in making his way through."

In penetrating walls there was no question that Spike, given the chance, would prove no less adept than an ivory-billed. He could drill a hole to freedom, window or no window. Even more perplexing to contemplate, he could bore a hole into the next room. And the next. And the next. There really was no limit. The walls of a house are minor obstacles in the path of a determined woodpecker.

Mrs. Tracy next placed Spike in a heavy plastic carrier of the sort used to transport dogs and cats on airplanes. In hopes of keeping him busy, she put in a stump and some small logs for him to drill.

In the days that followed Spike hammered incessantly. The logs in his cage were of absolutely no interest, but the walls of the enclosure made perfect sounding boards. If one stood nearby, the noise Spike produced was deafening. Elsewhere in the house it was merely obnoxious.

At night, mercifully, the red-headed percussionist slept soundly.

The Tracys grew tired of the racket and were worried that the bird, who as yet had shown no signs of breaking through the flexible plastic, might damage his beak. So they sought advice. Mrs. Tracy placed calls to several acquaintances who also worked with birds, including one on the staff of the Bronx Zoo. The response was unanimous: they laughed. No one could think of a secure, soundproof place to house a woodpecker.

The Bronx Zoo, Mrs. Tracy was told, had once faced a similar, although somewhat smaller, problem. They had tried to house a downy woodpecker, a bird about as close to Spike in size as a mouse is to a beaver. The little woodpecker was intended to be part of a lavish new habitat exhibit of American birds, but after being placed in the display, it pecked on everything in sight. In time the woodpecker proved so destructive to the costly backdrop that it was permanently removed.

However enlightening, the zoo's experience offered the Tracys little solace. They were disheartened, but out of their despair came an idea. Why not, they wondered, build Spike an "edible" cage? They could assemble a suitable enclosure of cheap lumber, and whenever Spike verged on escaping, they would simply nail on a few additional boards. It seemed the perfect solution: the cage would grow outward, and Spike could satisfy his urge to peck while his fractures healed.

Mr. Tracy bought an abundant supply of one-by-three pine furring and several pounds of nails. One Saturday afternoon, while the patient hammered on his plastic cage, the human hammered on the nails and boards. The duet undoubtedly raised the eyebrows of the wild woodpeckers in the Tracys' neighborhood, but it soon ended. The cage was about eight feet in height, four by six feet in cross section. Inside went lots of logs—and Spike.

The idea worked, at least for a while. Spike worked by day, Mr. Tracy by night, nailing on new boards over the places where the woodpecker's beak had inflicted the greatest damage. The cage grew. For a time, Spike and his keepers coexisted peaceably.

But as weeks passed, the bird's strength grew, nourished by the rich things Mrs. Tracy was feeding him: crickets, mealworms, dogfood, fruit. Soon it got so that Spike could blast his way out of confinement in fifteen minutes. One evening Mr. Tracy summed up the situation with Churchillian flair: "Never has so much one-by-three been consumed by so few in so short a time."

The banging of beak against wood was incessant. (I know because I heard it myself.) Callers who spoke with the Tracys by telephone during the edible-cage episode often inquired about the carpenters hammering in the background.

Meanwhile Spike, more interested in demolition than in construction, showed no signs of tiring and began to reveal certain interesting traits of personality. He started to call regularly, his voice a curious mix of riotous chuckles and laughter. Speech (if one can apply that term to his utterances) endowed Spike with individual character, but at the same time, from the Tracys' viewpoint, it made his presence more exasperating.

Spike proved impossible to photograph. In the wild, when a woodpecker sees a predator approaching, it vanishes. The trick is easily explained: the feathered Houdini sidesteps, quietly and without flapping its wings, to the side of the tree opposite its prospective enemy. If the predator moves, it moves. If the predator stays put, it stays put. Maintaining a shield of wood between itself and danger, a woodpecker can be as difficult to capture as a queen on a chessboard. Spike used this gambit to brilliant advantage. Whenever Mrs. Tracy entered his cage with a camera, he disappeared behind one of the logs Mr. Tracy had installed as perches.

At last—long last—Spike's bandages were ready to come off. Mrs. Tracy peeled away the surgical tape and was relieved to find her patient fully mended. The broken wing was strong again and it had healed in the proper position.

Now it was time to let Spike make a test flight indoors. Mrs. Tracy watched. Even though the bird hadn't been aloft in two months, his form seemed good. Of course, the only way to know for sure how well Spike could fly would be to release him. This seemed a reasonable thing to do. In every respect, Spike appeared to be strong, healthy, and ready for freedom.

The Tracys have released hundreds of birds, but to this day no departure has been as emotionally charged as was Spike's.

On one hand they were glad to rid themselves of the problematic woodpecker, but at the same time they would miss him. His hard-headed and independent character, his hysterical laugh, and his inexhaustible *joie de vivre* had touched them.

On a cool October day Spike was set free. He flapped across the Tracys' lawn, chuckling loudly as he flew, landed gracefully on a tulip tree, and immediately started drilling into the trunk. Slivers of wood fluttered to the ground.

A minute or so later, Spike flew into the woods and disappeared.

Spike visited the Tracys several times in the weeks that followed. Each time they saw him, Spike was in fine shape. He laughed, chiseled holes in trees in search of ants and grubs, and zipped through the air as if his accident had never happened.

When last I spoke with Mrs. Tracy, I posed a question. Would she and her husband ever again accept as a patient a pileated woodpecker? There was a long pause. Yes, probably, well, er, she said, they'd have to think about it.

8

Hummingbirds:
The Real Story

Popular books and magazine articles portray hummingbirds in glowing terms. In fact, the praise gets laid on so thick that one would think most of the accounts were written by mother hummingbirds. After all, it seems excessive to call any animal a "jewel," even if it does have a throat that sparkles red or blue or gold. Admittedly, no hummingbird is drab, and even in the dimmest light a feather-worn hummingbird manages to cut a striking figure. But to qualify as jewels I would expect the little monsters to exhibit civilized behavior.

Hummingbirds, you see, are bullies. Rocketing through the treetops at speeds of up to sixty miles per hour, their hearts pumping nearly 1,300 times each minute, hummingbirds are impatient and belligerent. They guard their favorite patches of red and violet trumpet-shaped flowers from their neighbors with the single-mindedness of knights defending virgins. Intruders beware: the hummingbird that blunders into another hummingbird's territory is playing with lightning.

Woe, too, to any other sort of bird that strays into a hummingbird's airspace. A few days ago at our house, a cardinal appeared at one of the two bird feeders that hang outside the kitchen window. This same cardinal had visited that feeder every day, morning and night, for months. On this particular occasion, however, the cardinal came, went, and so far has not returned.

The cardinal was stabbed by a hummingbird. The big red bird was perched, nibbling absentmindedly on sunflower seeds spread on a shelf feeder, when the hummingbird materialized at the adjacent nectar feeder, which was put out exclusively for hummingbirds. Without warning, the hummingbird buzzed sideways, covering the twenty-four inches between the two feeders in less time than it takes a politician to make a promise, and with his swordlike beak jabbed the unsuspecting cardinal in the belly.

Probably as much appalled by the hummingbird's lack of manners as pained by the physical insult it had sustained, the cardinal lingered on the feeder for half a minute, uttering sharp chips of irritation. Then it turned its back on our house and flapped away. Meanwhile the hummingbird went about its business, which consisted at that time of sucking gluttonously from our hummingbird feeder. Then it flew away, perhaps to drive off a neighbor or hunt for heartier fare. (Contrary to a widespread belief, hummingbirds are not vegetarians. The bulk—literally—of their diet consists of soft-bodied, utterly defenseless insects that the birds skewer and devour.)

At great speed a hummingbird can fly forward, backward, and sideways, and these abilities serve it well in catching insects. A few birds may fly more swiftly, but none can maneuver half as well as the hummer. However, for all its vaunted talents on the wing, a hummingbird is grounded at sundown. A hummingbird can no more fly at night than can a vampire (of the Bela Lugosi variety) roam the world at high noon.

Hummingbirds, you see, noctivate. At bedtime, when no one is looking, they settle on branches and shut down their engines. This *must* be done because hummingbirds, more wasteful of energy than vintage Cadillacs, perish quickly if they cannot eat. Every night, in other words, each hummingbird goes into a sort of short-term hibernation. Almost to the point of death, its heart rate and breathing slow, and its body heat drops from a normal setting of more than one hundred degrees to the temperature of the surrounding air.

Perhaps this peculiarity of hummingbird physiology will give our cardinal its chance for revenge. One night, perhaps, it will wait in a tree and watch to see where the hummingbird rests for the night. Then, one branch at a time, the bigger bird will move in, and when it reaches the hummingbird, it will lean over, pluck the inert hummingbird up by its beak, and shake it vigorously. Thus the cardinal may have the satisfaction of giving the little jewel a lesson in table manners.

9
The Roadrunner:
Clocking Cuckoos

*I*t paused at the brink for a moment, then jumped. The roadrunner flew with wings rigidly extended, not flapping but sailing like a man on a hang glider. Out over the desert it went, descending slowly in a nearly straight line, skimming over the top of a cholla cactus before touching down in the sand.

The flight began and ended in a matter of seconds, but the impression it left on me was lasting. Here was a different sort of bird, a bird that not only kills snakes and runs roads (behaviors for which the roadrunner of the American Southwest is famous), but steps blithely off precipices and glides through the air as if flapping were somehow beneath its dignity.

My wife Debbie and I had been seeing roadrunners often. Camping in Big Bend National Park, in rugged mountains called the Chisos that loom over the muddy Rio Grande, we had left our campsite at 5,300 feet and driven each day into the Chihuahuan desert. The desert, bitterly dry but inhabited by myriad wildflowers, shrubs, and cacti, surrounds the Chisos like a ditch encircling a fort. Here we examined dozens of the plants and animals that give the park its character, but to us the most interesting and engaging was the roadrunner.

The first roadrunner we saw was standing squarely in the middle of the U.S. highway that leads south into Big Bend from Marathon, Texas. The bird was pecking at a snake, or some other moribund reptile, that lay on the asphalt, and as we approached at fifty-five miles per hour it showed no intention of moving aside. In the end the roadrunner did not budge. Just before impact we veered. The roadrunner was saved from becoming one more roadside waffle, and we had learned something of its stubbornness.

In the days that followed, down by the Rio Grande in a floodplain, we saw roadrunners often. They kept pretty much clear of each other, wandering on long sturdy legs back and forth through the short grass. Occasionally one would stop to pluck a fat grasshopper or leap into the air to snap up a dragonfly. The most singular of the roadrunners spent nearly all of its time atop a picnic table, which it used as a sort of observation tower. If you walked near the table the bird would hop off, but a moment later it would be back. There were few territorial interactions that we could see, so Debbie and I assumed that the roadrunner was scrutinizing the greensward around its table for insects.

Roadrunners are placed by ornithologists in the cuckoo family. This makes them kin of the yellow-billed and black-billed cuckoos, two birds that between them inhabit nearly every forest from southern Canada to northern Mexico. The roadrunner, however, is strictly a resident of the Southwest. Here, when it is not standing on picnic tables, the roadrunner struts through the desert and chaparral in search of Tex-Mex specialties such as snakes, lizards, small birds, birds' eggs, mice, tarantulas, insects, and scorpions.

Looking at the roadrunners of Big Bend, we came to realize that the roadrunner is perhaps the handsomest of American cuckoos. At a glance its plumage is drab, like that of its wide-ranging relations, but on close inspection in good light, you can see an elegant olive sheen on the roadrunner's wings and central tail feathers, a jaunty crest that appears freshly coiffed, and a swath of pastel blue that runs through each eye and ends in a touch of crimson.

The roadrunner's most conspicuous feature, of course, is its preference for running rather than flying. Scientists have clocked these cuckoos at eighteen miles per hour, faster than the top speed of the average ornithologist but only about half the velocity of a hungry coyote. Apparently, whatever the roadrunner lacks in speed it makes up in wit and daring, for wherever you go in the southwestern states, you can usually be sure to find him.

10
Black Skimmers, or
"Sea Dogs"

To paraphrase George Orwell, all creatures are unique, but some are more unique than others. Among birds, the black skimmer may be the most unique of all.

The skimmer's distinctive features are numerous and striking. Most readily apparent is the underbite from which every adult black skimmer suffers. The bottom mandible of the beak juts out so much farther than the upper mandible that not even an orthodontist with a block and tackle could fix it. Interestingly, the underbite is absent in hatchling skimmers and develops only when the birds begin to fly.

No other American bird has seen fit to evolve a beak with the lower mandible longer than the upper, but the black skimmer makes the best of the situation. As it skims coastal waters from the North Atlantic to the Gulf of Mexico, the skimmer drags its peculiar lower mandible through the surface film and snaps up small fish and crustaceans. The mandible is sensitive to contact with even tiny morsels of food.

Length is not the only unusual aspect of the skimmer's lower mandible. Just as Englishmen evolved stiff upper lips to fit the rims of their teacups, skimmers developed fixed lower mandibles to aid in their skimming. (Usually, it is the upper mandible of a bird's beak that is fixed, while the lower is hinged and movable. But with skimmers the situation is reversed. The bottom half of the beak is fused to the skull, while the top mandible is lifted and lowered.) This arrangement may increase the skimmer's ability to sense floating prey as well as help it to withstand the jarring shocks that must occur from time to time when the mandible hangs up on something fixed and immovable.

The eye of the skimmer is also unique. Whereas other birds see the world through eyes with round pupils, black skimmers convey light to their retinas through vertical slits. If you can get close to a skimmer, look it in the eye and you will see an eye that would look at home on a cat or rattlesnake.

In terms of plumage, most birds appear to work hard at either trying to blend in with the colors and shapes of their environment or flashing bright colors to seduce females, intimidate rivals, or both. Skimmers take neither tack. They dress as if for the opera in elegant white and black. If penguins wear tuxedos, as is often said, skimmers, with their ebony-black wings that extend well beyond their rumps, step out in black tie and tails. A flock of skimmers winging its way across a bay at sunset as if hurrying to an evening performance of *Carmen* is one of the grandest sights in nature.

Even in bright light, a skimmer loses none of its dash. In fact, the vivid red of the skimmer's beak and legs, which can be seen only in good sun at close range, imparts a rakish touch. But the image falls apart when the skimmer speaks. Its strange calls are coarse, guttural, and not at all birdlike. To some, skimmers sound like barking hounds. Sailors call skimmers "sea dogs."

11
The Uncommon Crow

The plumage of the crow suggests, in dearth of color and blandness of style, the parlor garb of an undertaker. Yet catch a crow when the sun shines in just the right quarter, and you will see a familiar bird transformed. The common crow, in fact, is uncommonly handsome. His or her feathers shine. They are iridescent, reflecting, when sunlight does them justice, a natty blue, a deep sea green, or a rich glossy purple.

The crow, of course, is colorful in personality as well as plumage. He is mischievous. He will collect gold earrings and diamond rings and hoard them as a philatelist squirrels away stamps. One might fairly call him, by virtue of his pranks and his manner of skulking after food and treasure, a Peck's bad boy among birds.

It is an ancient schoolhouse tradition that bad boys like to pull hair, particularly when that hair is braided or pony-tailed and sprouts from the head of a girl. In days of yore when classroom desks harbored inkwells, a boy could achieve instant notoriety by dipping a girl's locks in the ink. Crows vary the human practice only slightly. They sneak up on mammals, particularly mammals larger than themselves, and yank on their tails.

A dangerous game? Certainly. But crows play it with gusto. The ornithologist Lawrence Kilham, during a research project in Florida, observed twenty-eight instances of crows tweaking the tails of otters. Only once did this act provide anything more than sport for the bird; on that occasion, the otter dropped its fish and the partner of the crow that had done the pulling made off with the prize. What explains the behavior? Kilham wondered if crows, in comparison to other birds, simply have more fun.

To fly through life with such panache the crow must be intelligent. Ornithologists, who often agree on few matters of substance, are virtually unanimous in proclaiming the crow the Einstein of American birds. Henry Ward Beecher, the nineteenth-century abolitionist, wrote that if men were fitted with wings and feathers, few would be sufficiently quick-witted to qualify as crows.

Support for the thesis of crow intelligence is abundant. Wildlife photographers, for example, have found that crows count. When three men enter a blind and two emerge, leaving the third man inside with a camera, most birds will think the coast is clear and go about their business. Crows, however, will know that the blind is occupied and refuse to venture near.

Crows are also considered intelligent because in communicating among themselves they utter a remarkable variety of cries, croaks, and gulps. The men and women who study crows have noted, recorded, and described twenty-three distinct crow calls. One is the familiar *caw*. Another sounds like the gobbling of a turkey. Still another, recorded in Florida by Kilham, is a bravura imitation of the barred owl.

A particularly compelling proof of crow perspicacity is a trick the birds have developed for opening nuts with hard shells. They drop the nuts, researchers in Florida observed, on busy roads. Automobile tires do the rest. What next? Who knows. It will be interesting to see what the crow thinks up for an encore.

The Winter Wren: Pavarotti of the Woodpile

A pile of firewood, carefully disorganized, attracts winter wrens in autumn the way cheese lures mice. Somewhere among the logs and empty spaces between them lurks a siren the little birds cannot resist.

As I walked to work one day, I saw a dark, fleeting shape out of the corner of my eye. It was hopping in and out of a wood heap I had dumped behind my house the night before. My eyes told me that the dusky figure darting to and fro among the logs was a mouse. But the setting and the season were suspicious. I decided to take a look.

When I approached within a few steps of the woodpile, the little animal jumped from its place and vanished, but not before I had made several observations. The "mouse" had a face that culminated not in whiskers and a furry nose but in a thin, pointed beak. Its body was the size of a golf ball, not uniformly brown as I had judged at first glance but crosshatched with fine lines, as if it had been sketched by an artist. The tail was distinctive. Decidedly unmouselike, it was short, stiff, and broad, cocked up and inclined toward the head. The picture was becoming clear. If the visitor to the woodpile was arrested for stealing insect larvae from beneath the bark of my logs, I could pick it from a police lineup. Airborne too long for a mouse, smaller and darker than a house wren, faster and more furtive than a sparrow, there was no doubt that the culprit was *Troglodytes troglodytes*, the winter wren.

Troglodytes, in ancient myth, are creatures of fable that live in caves. Applied to the bird, the name is apt. Winter wrens spend their lives seeking dark hollows. They find them in mossy banks, at the bases of trees behind curls of loose-fitting bark, between rocks, and deep among the roots of standing and overturned trees. In these wren-scale caves they nest in summer, roost in winter, and hunt for soft, wriggling creatures the year round.

During the cold months, winter wrens fling their procreative duties aside and take flight for warmer climes. When they do so, they carry their cave-affinity with them. Favorite haunts along the migratory routes of winter wrens are woodpiles, stone walls, old foundations, talus slopes, and the tangled branches of fallen trees. Most of the winter wrens I've come upon casually—those not sought out during birdwatching forays, but discovered by chance while I was engaged in other pursuits—have been seen darting along the faces of walls and woodpiles. At first each of these birds was glimpsed out of the corner of an eye and thought to be a rodent or shrew until, upon further observation and reflection, the dark shape became an unidentified flying object and gave the game away.

When winter wrens aren't busy looking like mice, they sing. Gilbert White, England's Thoreau, noted in his *Natural History of Selborne* that "wrens sing all the winter through, frost excepted." White, who stuck to his home ground as faithfully as his Massachusetts counterpart, was familiar with *Troglodytes troglodytes* because, unlike its cousin wrens who remained faithful to their family's New World origins, the winter wren set off from its homeland and explored, invaded, and colonized the European continent, England, and Asia. The North American winter wren and the bird known to White and the English simply as "the wren" are one and the same.

Frosts are more common in the *New* England than they are in the old. Following White's formula, this may explain why American winter wrens sing mainly in spring and summer. When a winter wren sings, everyone listens. To my ears the vocal performance of the little troglodyte is the most thrilling of all bird songs. Uttering a staccato burst of bell-like notes, the winter wren races up and down and all over the scale with breathtaking virtuosity. The song goes on and on and on. One would never expect that such a small, drab bird could have such a big and colorful voice. (Although a winter wren's performance seems to last forever, a person with a watch can spoil the fun and show that the entire symphony lasts only about six or seven seconds.)

John James Audubon, one of the first European-descended Americans to sing the winter wren's praises, described the vocal delivery of the bird as "energetic and melodious." "The song," he wrote, ". . . acts so powerfully on the mind as to inspire a feeling of wonder and delight." Hear a winter wren yourself and you may accuse Audubon of understatement.

F. Schuyler Mathews, author of the classic *Field Book Of Wild Birds And Their Music,* called the winter wren's singing "glorious" and described it as a "dancing melody [which] reverberates through the spruce forests like the tinkling of silver bells."

I write these words in autumn. Spring must come again before I can hear the singer who earned these raves. But in the meantime, whenever I desire to see the Pavarotti of the woodpile in his quiet moments, I need only find a stack of firewood and wait.

13

Peculiar Habits of the
Turkey Vulture

Had Emily Post not led such a sheltered life, she might have stepped outdoors more often, and there, in the untidy, unmannered, uncouth, unabashed world of nature she might have met a turkey vulture. Without a doubt, the doyenne of etiquette would have been appalled.

The reasons are numerous. When a turkey vulture sits down beside a carcass, the inside of which has turned to putrid slime, it wastes no time choosing the correct fork or putting a napkin on its lap. The bird simply plunges its head and neck into the meal and eats until it is gorged. Fortunately, evolution has provided the turkey vulture with a naked head, so after it has dipped repeatedly into a meal of vintage roadkill there is little need to clean up with soap and water. What little slime clings to the bird's bare skin after a meal is removed by helpful flies or simply dries and falls off in flakes.

Now comes the disgusting part. If a turkey vulture has youngsters to care for, it flies, belly full, back to its nest and regurgitates the meal into the mouths of its babes. Whether the young birds appreciate such fare—not exactly gourmet material the first time around, let alone the second—is difficult to ascertain. Perhaps they do not, which would explain why turkey vultures spend the rest of their lives roosting together in arboreal support groups.

On hot days, the turkey vulture employs a unique means of cooling itself. It urinates on its legs, and the evaporating excretion carries away excess heat. Apparently the procedure works reliably, for in a telephone survey of hospital emergency room personnel I was unable to find a single doctor or intern who could recall treating a vulture for heat prostration.

Turkey vultures also have a habit of defecating on their feet. "Why not," you might say, considering where their feet have been. By lifestyle alone the vulture seems far removed from concerns of personal hygiene. But the act is purposeful. It seems that the digestive juices of turkey vultures contain antibacterial and antiviral substances strong enough to kill just about any pathogen. Although Emily Post might have fainted to witness the act, a vulture soils its feet in order to keep healthy. The droppings kill germs. In a fashion, the turkey vulture is simply washing its hands.

Since turkey vultures keep pretty much to themselves, we rarely have a chance to witness their excretory and sanitary behavior. However, if one day you are lucky enough to approach a vulture up close, you may observe firsthand their most singular habit of all. When threatened or captured, a turkey vulture behaves something like an opossum or a hognose snake. It will suddenly go limp, pretending to be dead. Sometimes, however, for reasons known only to the bird, the vulture will opt not to play dead. Instead, it employs a method of self-defense more effective in repelling attackers than karate or kung fu.

It vomits.

The projectile vomiting of a turkey vulture is a weapon to be reckoned with, especially considering the bird's diet. *Foul* is too mild a word to describe the result. Certainly, any man or beast that approaches a turkey vulture too closely will not repeat the mistake.

14
The Wild Turkey:
Return of the Native

A half-hour before sunup, I opened the back door of my house as quietly as its creakiness would allow and stepped into the last hour of night. It was dark and frosty, and I could hear wind rattling frozen twigs in the treetops. Instantly I felt chilled. Somewhere out in the gloom I hoped to find early spring wildflowers dressed in wisps of photogenic frost. But I would have to hurry. The April sun would rise soon, spoiling my opportunities.

The right half of my brain demanded that I turn around and go back to bed; the left insisted that I forge ahead. This time the left side won. Clutching in one hand a cup of coffee that was fast losing its heat and cradling a camera in the other, I trudged halfheartedly into the coming day.

Gobble-gobble-gobble. What was that? A strange, guttural, far-off sound. Unfamiliar. Perhaps I was hearing things. I was still groggy from a 4:30 reveille; an early riser I am not. I walked away from the house, up the gravel driveway, and out to the road. In all directions meadows lay before me, each glazed white with a heavy frost that looked like snow. I walked east, straight toward the imminent sunrise.

Gobble-gobble-gobble. The sound came again. This time I was sure it was real. *Gobble-gobble-gobble.* The intervals between the calls (each was a loud, throaty rattle) were growing shorter and they seemed to convey a mounting urgency. *Gobble-gobble-gobble.* What on earth could it be? I had never before heard this noise. At the same time, the sound was familiar and I felt foolish for not recognizing it. I racked my brain. Surely this was the call of a bird. But *what* bird?

As the answer was surfacing in my awakening mind, I happened to look up and there, in full view, was the sound maker.

Of course! My confusion suddenly made perfect sense. I had known this sound since kindergarten, yet at the same time it was entirely new to me.

A quarter-century earlier, my kindergarten teacher, Miss Toye (Kaye Toye, as she was known to her colleagues), had introduced me to the bird during my first November of formal education. The gobbling of turkeys was, and I suppose will always be, as familiar to American schoolchildren as George Washington's cherry tree. Kids learn to gobble almost before they learn to talk. But this was the first gobbling of nonhuman origin ever to fall upon my ears, and I was eager to hear more of it.

The tom turkey was busily strutting and fanning his magnificent tail a hundred yards upslope, *gobbling* at intervals. But suddenly he stopped calling and looked in my direction. If I guessed correctly, the bird was struggling to reconcile powerful urges that had begun to pull in opposing directions. Should he run like hell, as turkeys generally do, at the sight of a human being, or should he continue to serenade his harem lurking in the bushes? Admittedly, it was a tough call.

Luckily for me, lust won over caution. The big tom stayed, *gobbled*, and *gobbled* some more while the sun rose behind him. I was captivated. Here, complete with the obligatory beard and banded tail, the plump torso and the scaly face, was a childhood drawing come alive. The turkey worked slowly across the meadow, calling and displaying his broad tail with an earnestness that made me laugh. Paralleling his course, I moved along the base of the hill, keeping close.

The most striking thing about the bird, once one looked beyond the tail which he regularly opened and closed to great dramatic effect, was his beard. It was long and scraggly and gave the turkey the air of an old patriarch. But the similarity was only superficial. The turkey's behavior was sexually charged, suggesting not a patriarch but a hot-blooded Casanova.

At first the turkey struck me as ugly. His head and neck were colored a cadaverous blue-white, and they were covered by skin that was warty and featherless, as if the bird had come down with a pox. I could see why Thomas Jefferson and John Adams had outvoted Benjamin Franklin and made the bald eagle our national symbol. Turkeys have a certain homely charm, but judging by the specimen in front of me, I could see that the species would win no avian beauty contest.

I remembered reading in a translation of Adriaen Van der Donck's 1655 *A History of New Netherland* that the wild turkeys found by seventeenth-century Dutch settlers were "large, heavy, fat and fine." Van der Donck's use of the word *fine* suggests, I think, that he had more than a passing interest in the shape and size of American turkeys. The turkey before me, which was well stuffed around the middle, would have made a fine meal for any man or beast.

Still following the turkey, I noticed that his contour feathers (those that cloak a bird's torso, following the contours of its body) were not lobed or butterknife-shaped, as they are on most birds, but were wide, squared off, and edged in black. Each contour feather overlapped the one below, and together they looked like shingles on a roof. Until dawn the feathers appeared a dull bronze, but as the sun rose, an iridescent sheen on them became apparent. The bird that had seemed plain and ugly only moments before suddenly radiated vivid blues, golds, and greens.

As he struts and gobbles, a successful tom may have as few as two or three or as many as a dozen hens watching nearby, willing to surrender their virtue. I wondered what sort of luck my bird was having this April morning. The hens, if there were any, never came into view.

Only a few years earlier, a tom turkey in my home woods could have gobbled around the clock for weeks and had no luck at all. Turkeys of both sexes disappeared from the area (and from most of the Northeast) around 1800, victims of the clearing of land for agriculture and early American appetites for fresh wildfowl. To the knowledge of local experts, no turkeys nested successfully in the area until 1985, although for several years before that, a lone hen had appeared every spring, laid a clutch of sterile eggs, and incubated them devotedly. (Bird-watchers nicknamed this bird the "Virgin Mary.") In 1985, several miles from the haunts of Mary, a hen was seen repeatedly with twelve gangly poults in tow, marching across the meadows of a nature preserve. Somewhere, somehow, a tom and a hen had managed to find each other.

And I'm pleased to report, toms and hens have been finding each other here ever since.

A car roared along the road behind me. The added disturbance was more than the amorous tom could bear. He folded his tail, ran a few steps, and leaped into the air like Superman. As the turkey gained altitude with long pumping wingbeats, I was struck by his ease in the air. He flew with grace.

After banking a wide turn, the turkey flew into the woods and disappeared. I set off for home. I hadn't got far, hadn't found the ice crystals and spring flowers I was searching for. But I *had* learned that turkeys really do gobble, just as Miss Toye said they did.

15

Northern Orioles: A Mystery Solved

On a sunny June morning, a pair of orioles perched on the lowest branch of a maple tree near my house, screaming at something. Perhaps they had spied a snake or a weasel that was hidden from my view by the tall grass. I visited the spot, but to my surprise, neither snake nor weasel was to be seen. In fact, *nothing* was there. Yet the orioles returned immediately and resumed their clamor, which was undoubtedly a great drain on their energy.

Why the fuss? It undoubtedly had something to do with the fledglings, fresh out of the nest, that were cowering in a nearby bush. The parents had invested much effort in weaving their nest, filling it with eggs, incubating the eggs, and brooding and feeding the young, and they were not about to let a predator fill its stomach without a fight.

But where was the predator? The orioles had a definite location in mind, directly beneath the low branch. Yet as I have already mentioned, there was nothing there save grass, a few prickly thistles, one or two horse nettles, and some debris left behind by the previous tenant of my house. It was a mystery worthy of Arthur Conan Doyle, and I was determined to solve it rather than spend the rest of the week wondering what had been going on. Because my earlier, active search for clues had proved fruitless, I decided to wait and watch, reasoning that sooner or later I would either have a Holmesian brainstorm or the birds would give the game away.

At noon the confrontation was still in full swing. The parent orioles, the striking black-and-orange male and the soft pastel female, both now ragged of voice, were hopping fretfully along the limb, looking groundward and uttering strident cries. The young orioles cowered in the same bush. Again I investigated, and again I found nothing.

At mid-afternoon the parent birds were *still* obsessed with the ground beneath the branch, and having grown increasingly weary of waiting passively, I vowed to search the area once more for clues. I knew enough about the behavior of wild birds in general to be sure that orioles recognize genuine enemies when they see them. (Even nestlings fresh from the egg shrink in fear when a hawk, owl, or crow passes overhead.) The orioles would not be wasting precious time and energy scolding something or someone unless it posed—or appeared to pose— a threat. Conclusion: in my earlier sleuthing, I had missed something.

I visited the area again. This time the predator jumped out at me, at least figuratively. It was a length of old rubber garden hose, black and about four feet long, half buried in the thatch of last year's grass cuttings. Unless I missed my guess, the orioles, a bit jumpy with their young so fresh out of the nest, had mistaken the hose for a black rat snake, the nemesis of all tree-nesting birds. Black rat snakes climb to great heights to devour songbirds. Once I climbed into the upper branches of a beech tree to investigate a ruckus I had heard and found two angry rose-breasted grosbeaks, an empty nest, and an unrepentant rat snake with three telltale lumps in its midriff.

To test my garden hose theory, I relocated the "snake" to a trash can across the road. Then, at a comfortable distance, I sat down on the grass and waited.

The orioles returned to the branch. This time, looking down and finding nothing, they were satisfied. The male perched and sang triumphantly, the female flew to the fledglings in the bush, and during the rest of the day a busy calm prevailed. Meanwhile, I crawled into bed that night quite pleased with myself, wishing only that Dr. Watson had been on hand to record my triumph.

PART TWO

Fur and Wide

1
Never Underestimate
an Opossum

Among naturalists, it is traditional to look condescendingly upon the slow-moving, ratlike opossum. In books and journals, the opossum carries more than its share of pejoratives, all reinforcing the general idea that the animal is stupid and primitive. At last, however, opinion may be changing. A recent article in *Scientific American* by biologist Stephen Austad suggests that opossums deserve better treatment. In a study designed to examine the ability of various animals to recall the location of food sources, Austad reports, only humans outperformed opossums. Dogs, cats, pigs, goats, rats, and rabbits—all widely supposed to be brighter than opossums—came up short. Austad stops well short of labeling the opossum an Einstein among mammals, but he does suggest that in matters of intelligence the opossum is anything but a dimwit.

And a keen ability to find and relocate food is not the only thing the opossum has going for it, Austad points out. Opossums are immune to the venom of North American pit vipers—rattlesnakes, copperheads, and cottonmouths—and are unique in that they can feed on these snakes with impunity. Opossums are also exceptionally efficient in the business of manufacturing offspring. Mother opossums raise two, sometimes three, litters of six, seven, or eight young in a single year. A high birthrate is necessary because opossums have lots of predators and even under the best of conditions die of old age at the age of two.

Opossums are marsupials. Like kangaroo joeys, young opossums pass their infancy in a pouch on their mother's belly, there enjoying milk, warmth, safety, and complimentary transportation. Paleontologists think that marsupials probably originated in the Americas, not in Australia as is widely supposed. The oldest known marsupial fossils have been found in Canada and the western United States. Of great antiquity, they date to a time when tyrannosaurus, stegosaurus, and hundreds of other dinosaurs still ruled the earth.

Marsupial ancestors of the opossum dispersed across the globe. A few reached Europe, Africa, and Asia, although they are extinct in these places today. Some reached Australia, where their descendants now flourish. Of the world's 266 living marsupial species, 120 are native Australians.

The North American opossum is as remarkable as any of its famed Southern Hemisphere cousins. Among its many notable traits is a habit of feigning death ("playing 'possum") when frightened, a ruse which can confuse a predator and spare the opossum's life. Sometimes, however, playing 'possum can be carried to a dangerous extreme. I know of an opossum that was found motionless beneath some boards when an old shed was demolished. The finder, a young man who was compassionate toward animals, even dead ones, knew little about opossum behavior. He took the "dead" opossum, a Lawrence Olivier of its species, to a secluded spot and there, with the best of intentions, did for it what he had done for other animal corpses he had encountered in his work and travels: he buried it.

The story is ghastly but bears recounting because it points to an important lesson. In acting ability as in other attributes, *never* underestimate an opossum.

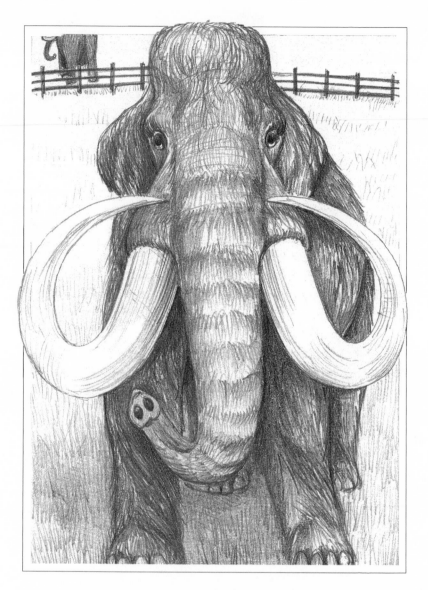

2
Mammoths and Mastodons: Better Lawn Mowers

If you could convert your home into a time machine and turn back the clock twelve thousand years, you might look out the kitchen window one morning while making coffee and spy an elephant grazing on the lawn. It would be a large elephant, taller and heavier than any you have seen at a zoo. Its body would be covered in fur—thick and shaggy fur like that of a yak. The beast would sport a trunk, of course, a great curving proboscis as big around as a fireman's hose. And there would be tusks.

The tusks would be striking. Long, twisted near the ends, and as thick as the end of a baseball bat, the tusks in their extravagant massiveness would make you wonder how the elephant could ever raise its head. (Speaking of the head, on top of the elephant's there would be a conspicuous lump, as if the animal, wearing some sort of hairy, brimless cap, were on its way to a lodge meeting.) You would be looking at a mammoth, genus *Mammuthus*, a type of elephant that lived during the Pleistocene, a period of frequent ice ages. The Pleistocene ended about ten thousand years ago; you and your time machine have caught the tail end.

At least three varieties of mammoth roamed the Ice Age tundra and grasslands of North America. The smallest, which was significantly bigger than any elephant alive today, was the most abundant. It had no English or Latin name in its own time, but today, retroactively, we call it the woolly mammoth.

Even without time machines, we have a pretty good idea of what woolly mammoths looked like. Skeletons have been unearthed, and it has been found that their bones are not much different from those of modern elephants. Scientists infer that mammoths were generally elephantlike in shape and stature. Because entire specimens—flesh, fur, and all—have been exhumed from permafrost in the far north, we also know that woolly mammoths were covered in thick fur and that this fur was probably red-brown in color.

To cite a recent find, on June 23, 1977, a baby woolly mammoth was freed from permafrost near the Kirgilyakh River, in Siberia. The little elephant had been dead for 40,000 years, experts estimated, but its carcass was in fine condition (better, perhaps, than yours or mine). You can see this mammoth with your own eyes, if you wish, by visiting it at the natural history museum in St. Petersburg, formerly Leningrad.

We also know how woolly mammoths looked because some of the people who hunted them in Europe during the Stone Age took the time to draw and scratch their likenesses on the walls of caves. One of the best of these images, an engraving in the cave of *les Combarelles* near Les Eyzies in the Dordogne, France, depicts a complete mammoth profile. The shaggy coat, oversized tusks, and domed head are clearly visible.

A cohabitant of the woolly mammoth in North America during the Pleistocene was Jefferson's mammoth. This animal, slightly larger than the woolly mammoth, seems to have ranged farther to the south. Jefferson's mammoth was named for Thomas Jefferson, the most ardent paleontologist among our presidents. (Jefferson commissioned Lewis and Clark to explore the West for a variety of reasons, one of which was a keen interest in knowing if living mammoths existed in the vast wilderness beyond the Appalachians.) Inside the White House, Jefferson set aside a room for the exhibition of bones. Included in his display were the skeletal remains of North American elephants. Several bones from a Jefferson's mammoth were dug from a swamp near Ossining, New York, in 1961. One of these, a thighbone I once had the pleasure of holding in my arms, was nearly six feet in length.

The imperial mammoth, close cousin to the woolly and the Jefferson's, was the largest elephant or elephantlike creature ever to roam the earth. Imperial in every respect, it had a range that included Europe, Asia, Africa, and North America.

Return to the window and watch the elephant on your lawn closely. If it is content to graze on crabgrass and is not soon joined by other elephants, it is probably a mammoth of one sort or another. But if other elephants appear, and they soon begin to devour your azaleas, you have probably been looking at a mastodon. Mastodons, distant cousins of the mammoths and our modern elephants, moved in groups. They fed on woody plant material—twigs, bark, and branches. The name mastodon means "breastlike teeth" and refers to the fact that each mastodon molar has a pair of Dolly Parton–shaped cones projecting from its chewing surface. When the mastodon was alive, these aided in pulverizing food.

Mammoths, on the other hand, traveled alone and fed on grasses and herbs. Scientists know this because mammoth skeletons are generally found singly and because the stomachs of frozen mammoths contain the remains of grasses, sedges, and wildflowers. Mammoth teeth had fairly smooth grinding surfaces. In hand, a mammoth molar, heavy and flat on the chewing surface, suggests a rather substantial fragment of a millstone.

If you live in the suburbs and think deer are great pests in your yard and garden, be thankful there are no longer any mastodons. Of course, if you abhor cutting the grass, start praying for another ice age; perhaps the mammoth, a lawn mower without equal, will return and put Toro and Lawn Boy out of business.

3
The Woodchuck, or Whistle Pig

How much wood
Could a woodchuck chuck
If a woodchuck could chuck wood?
—An old rhyme

One day, a naturalist will come along who will trumpet the virtues of the woodchuck. But the wait may be long. The woodchuck is chubby and clumsy; it digs holes—lots of them—in pastures where farm animals graze and unwittingly is the cause among horses and cattle of many a broken femur; and it raids gardens. I know of luckless suburbanites whose entire backyard vegetable patches have been sacrificed in expanding a woodchuck's waistline, and I know peace-loving men and women who were driven by exasperation to raise axe and shovel against the woodchuck.

The woodchuck is a marmot (*Marmota monax* is its scientific name), and marmots are prodigious eaters. They move across meadows slowly and inexorably, like hot-blooded glaciers, consuming everything tasty in their paths. America is home to three marmot species—in the West, the hoary marmot and the yellow-bellied marmot, and in the East the woodchuck, or groundhog. All three marmots possess pumpkin-colored incisor teeth that cut plant stems with remarkable efficiency.

Eating is a sport at which the woodchuck excels. (It is not called ground*hog* for nothing.) Consuming sixteen ounces of food at a single meal is not unusual—a significant feat for an animal that typically weighs only five or ten pounds. Given the chance, a woodchuck, like any gourmand, will put on fat as determinedly as a miser accumulates money. The biggest woodchucks known from the wild weigh in the neighborhood of fifteen pounds, but a few have grown heavier. A well-fed captive specimen once tipped the scales at a shocking thirty-nine pounds!

Well-stuffed though it may be, the woodchuck is still a squirrel, and it proves the point from time to time by climbing trees. The first time I saw a woodchuck out on a limb I could hardly believe my eyes. It looked like a miniature Goodyear blimp that, upon getting its hawsers tangled in the branches, had responded by sprouting a coat of hair. What do wood-chucks do in trees? The old rhyme notwithstanding, they do not chuck wood. A woodchuck gets in an arboreal mood because some fruit it covets is ripening or some bud is swollen, and it cannot resist the temptation to climb and consume.

Arboreal adventures notwithstanding, it is on (and under) the ground that the woodchuck is really at home. Here it does most of its eating. Here, before resuming the solitary life which is traditional for woodchucks, it consorts briefly with Mrs. Woodchuck. And here it digs, and digs, and digs some more until its burrow system is vast and labyrinthine. A woodchuck's burrow contains all the comforts. Inside there is a toilet cham-ber for defecating; a bedroom for midday siestas and winter hibernation; assorted passageways (some cul-de-sacs, others leading to auxiliary ports of escape and entry); and if the premises belong to a mature female, a nursery. As wild animals go, woodchucks are fastidious housekeepers. Look at the entrance to a burrow and nearby you will generally find a pile of sweepings—dirt, dust, droppings, and so forth. It is not unusual for a woodchuck to scrape out its burrow several times a week.

When a woodchuck is not cleaning house, eating, or sleep-ing, it is doing its roly-poly best to avoid predators. A fat mar-mot makes a splendid meal for a fox, hawk, or farm dog, and the woodchuck knows it. Its repertoire of responses to danger, however, is limited; occasionally the woodchuck stands and fights, but generally it whistles loudly and bolts for the burrow.

Whistling woodchucks? Yes. In some places the locals, familiar with both the alarm call and the appetite of the beast, call the woodchuck the "whistle pig." It is hard to imagine a better name for a marmot that eats and squeals like bacon on the hoof.

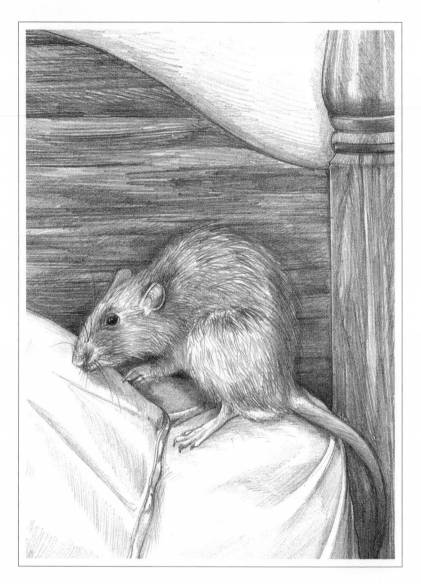

Norway Rats: Mammals that Won the World

What mammal, radiating outward from a point of origin somewhere in Eurasia, colonized all the continents and nearly every island on earth? What animal travels far and wide on land, swims and dives capably in water, enjoys seafood, fresh fowl, and home-grown vegetables, and belongs to a group that the paleontologist Robert Carroll calls "the most successful of all mammals"? What highly intelligent, highly social mammal could best write a travel manual titled *A Hitchhiker's Guide to Planet Earth?*

The answer to all three riddles is a rodent that people outside of Norway call the Norway rat. *Rattus norvegicus* (the scientific name is simply a reversal of the common), a cosmopolitan creature today, originated in the Old World, although its exact homeland no one can say. Some experts believe that Norway rats evolved in northern China or Mongolia, others that they first appeared along the Caspian Sea. Either way, long before the birth of Alexander the Great, the Norway rat began to conquer the world.

Like another prolific and widespread mammal we know (hint: a two-legged ape with a fondness for hamburgers, sushi, and ice cream), the Norway rat was well suited for conquest. Behaviorally as well as anatomically it is a generalist, able and willing, as conditions necessitate, to swim, crawl, climb, burrow, fight, retreat, cooperate, or go it alone. Its diet is catholic—under conditions hospitable or otherwise, the Norway rat can eat and thrive upon just about anything, including live animals, corpses, vegetables, and its own offspring. When pressed, Norway rats have even been known to snatch flesh from large animals that were sleeping. "We have seen both adults and children," wrote John James Audubon in *Quadrupeds of North America*, "who, by their wanting a piece of the ear, or a bit of the end of the nose, bore painful testimony to [the Norway rat's] having attacked them while they were in bed."

To cross vast oceans and reach lands as remote from its Eurasian homeland as England, the Americas, Hawaii, Australia, and New Zealand, the Norway rat stowed away on ships. It did so probably by accident; the rat followed mooring ropes out to ships, discovered food supplies and hiding places, and set up housekeeping. When the ships sailed, the rats, having no advance warning of the departure, sailed with them.

Not long after the rats first swam ashore in the British Isles during the eighteenth century, a scientist captured one of them, identified it as a new species, and figuring that the rats had arrived on ships from Oslo or Bergen, christened it the Norway rat. In a matter of decades, seafaring Norway rats swarmed ashore at virtually every outpost of European civilization. In North America they arrived around the time that Paul Revere took his midnight ride.

Today there are few places on earth where Norway rats cannot be found. In the Arctic, in the tropics, and most places in between, they thrive and multiply. Prospects for additional range expansion are now limited by geography, but one day perhaps, if Norway rats hitch rides on spaceships to Mars, one of earth's most intelligent and adaptive animals will begin scurrying toward new horizons.

5
Flying Squirrels: With the Greatest of Ease

n the lyrics of an old circus song, a daring young man sails through the air with the greatest of ease. Each night, perhaps only a hundred feet from where you sleep, a flying squirrel may do the same, gliding through the darkness for 25, 75, or 125 feet until it bends its tail, tilts its flattened body, and thumps squarely onto a tree trunk. The feat is performed again and again until sunrise. Then, about the same time your alarm clock is going off, the flying squirrel retires to its lair in a hollow tree, not to rise again until nightfall.

Because they are active only under cover of darkness, flying squirrels are rarely heard and almost never seen, even though in many woods they outnumber all other kinds of squirrels. This is a pity. Flying squirrels are handsome creatures, and they are a pleasure to watch in flight.

There are two ways to observe flying squirrels: by happening upon one or by engaging in a little old-fashioned planning and patience. To go the serendipitous route, consult a library book or a naturalist and make sure that the animals inhabit your part of the country; then venture into a woodland at dusk or after dark and gaze intently among the trees. If luck is with you, a flying squirrel may sail into your range of vision. You will recognize it because, rather than flap through the air like a bat or bird, the squirrel glides effortlessly like a Frisbee. Chances of success with this strategy are fair to good, and they get better the longer you wait.

A more reliable method for seeing these big-eyed, chipmunk-size squirrels is to search by day for telltale signs of their feeding or nesting, and then to return by night to the places where you've found such evidence. The key to this technique is knowing what to look for. Flying squirrels eat, among other things, great numbers of nuts. They're especially partial to those of hickories, walnuts, and butternuts. All of these trees produce fruits with soft, edible portions protected by thick woody husks. To snack on the inner kernels, the flying squirrel must gnaw one or more holes through the husks. This they accomplish with sharp front teeth, which are protected like the incisors of other rodents by a hard orange enamel.

A flying squirrel tackles the job of opening a nut with precision. Holding a nut in its delicate front paws, the squirrel bores into the husk, cutting one or more round (or egg-shaped) holes that penetrate to the inner chamber. The holes made in nuts by flying squirrels have smooth, polished edges. Other squirrels tackle the task in their own fashion. Gray squirrels chew the husk on the side too, but the holes they make are larger than those of the flying squirrels and are rough around the edges. (Often a gray squirrel will demolish a husk, leaving only fragments.) Red squirrels open nuts not from the sides but from the ends.

Thus, with a little sleuthing, you can locate nuts that have been opened by flying squirrels. You rarely have to look far for evidence. Flying squirrels throw away empties with the same abandon that certain larger, noisier animals discard beer cans.

When searching a woods for squirrel spoor, it's a good idea to keep an eye out for possible nest holes. If opened nuts are abundant in a particular spot, an active den is probably nearby. Don't look for conspicuous nests of dried leaves; these are most likely the work of gray squirrels. Look instead for old woodpecker holes (round openings in tree trunks) fairly high off the ground—twenty feet up, say, or higher. If an opening is clear and there are no spiderwebs or cocoons clinging to its edges, an animal of some sort is probably using it. The inhabitant may be the original builder (one of several species of woodpecker), a flying squirrel, or if you're really lucky, a whole acrobatic troupe of flying squirrels. Then again, the hole may belong to a screech owl, a great crested flycatcher, or a chickadee. There's no simple way to tell.

But wait and watch the hole in the tree long enough, and you'll discover who's inside. Flying squirrels emerge from active dens after sundown. Usually their scurrying out produces only a faint scraping of claws against bark, although at times I've heard rousing squirrels utter high-pitched peeps and squeals, or gentle noises barely audible over the other sounds of the woods.

When they emerge, flying squirrels often ascend into their host tree's upper branches. They are not graceful climbers. The loose folds of skin the squirrels carry at their sides seem encumbrances. Yet they climb capably, and have little trouble reaching the crowns of the tallest oaks and maples.

From high in a tree, a flying squirrel launches itself into the air like a skydiver jumping from an airplane. As it becomes airborne, the little animal stretches out its fore- and hind legs, and the loose flaps of skin on its flanks open into an elegant and effective parachute. Silently, the squirrel plunges through the darkness like a gigantic snowflake. Its tail, flatter than those of other squirrels, works like a rudder, guiding the descent.

Flying squirrels, the experts say, are not true fliers. Nor are hang gliders fliers, if flight is defined narrowly as a lengthy and self-sustaining journey through the atmosphere. Yet having flown a hang glider myself and experienced the blended states of ecstasy and terror that make the sport so appealing, I would argue that the aerial exploits of flying squirrels and glider pilots constitute "flying" just as much as those of birds, bats, and airplanes. Granted, airborne squirrels and hang gliders can't remain aloft indefinitely. But then neither can pelicans and B-52s, no matter how large their jowls or fuel tanks.

When you finally observe a flying squirrel in action, you may have to settle for a momentary glimpse. It is not unusual for a squirrel to vanish into the darkness as swiftly and unexpectedly as it appeared. Only occasionally does one get a lengthy view.

On one such occasion, a group of graduate students from the film school at New York University were shooting a night scene in the yard of my house. The house stood in the middle of a nature sanctuary, and when I first inhabited it the attic was visited nightly by flying squirrels. (Although I never saw the squirrels, I found their droppings and heard their squeals and scratchings.) Late one afternoon a crew arrived and unloaded a truck filled with cameras, tripods, sound equipment, thick electric cables, and enormous floodlights. The filming began just after dark. While two actors portraying feuding brothers staged a heated argument on my porch, I stood on a knoll a hundred yards away, watching from the shadows. The glare of the floodlights filtered up through the three old sugar maples that grew in the yard, and as I glanced into the illuminated branches, I found that another drama, spontaneous and unscripted, was also taking place.

Three flying squirrels were winging silently back and forth, unseen by the actors and technical crew below them. Were the animals disturbed by the commotion in their territory, reveling in the limelight, or simply going about their nightly routine? I couldn't be sure. Whatever the case, zipping to and fro at great speed, the squirrels appeared to be having a ball. And so was I—a finer acrobatic display has never been staged.

Although the antics of flying squirrels are a treat to observe in an appropriate open-air venue, they can seem less than charming when they occur in an attic or bedroom. Squirrels of any sort in any house can be noisy, but flying squirrels are so active they'll literally bounce off the walls of a room, night after night, without any consideration for the humans who may be sleeping (or trying to) nearby. The naturalist John Burroughs once received a rude reminder of the flying squirrel's least enduring trait during a visit with President Theodore Roosevelt and his family in the spring of 1908. Burroughs had come to visit the Roosevelts at their rustic retreat at Pine Knot, Virginia. He stayed in a bedroom that, as it turned out, was already occupied.

Roosevelt tells the story in a letter dated May 10, 1908, sent from the White House to his son Archie:

> Mother and I had great fun at Pine Knot. Mr. Burroughs, whom I call Oom John, was with us and we greatly enjoyed having him. But one night he fell into great disgrace! The flying squirrels that were there last Christmas had raised a brood, having built a large nest inside of the room in which . . . John Burroughs slept. Of course they held high carnival at night-time. Mother and I do not mind them at all, and indeed rather like to hear them scrambling about. . . . But one night they waked up John Burroughs and he spent a misguided hour hunting for the nest, and when he found it took it down and caught two of the young squirrels and put them in a basket. The next day under Mother's direction I took them out, getting my fingers somewhat bitten in the process, and loosed them in our room. . . . I do not think John Burroughs profited by his misconduct, because the squirrels were more active than ever that night, both in his room and ours. . . .

Sharing a bedroom with flying squirrels, Burroughs discovered, can be more ordeal than adventure. Sharing a woodland with them, however, is another matter. The squirrels pay no attention to people, and people, for the most part, pay no attention to the squirrels. The arrangement—one of peaceful coexistence—has long proved felicitous for both parties, and as a result, flying squirrels—there are two species, the northern and the southern—inhabit the forests of North America in great numbers.

6
The Porcupine:
Handle With Care

Porcupines are pests. Under cover of darkness, they gnaw tool handles, cut fishing poles into lengths, and sever the hydraulic brake lines of automobiles. Nevertheless, porcupines must be credited with an abundance of positive points.

First, they are easy-going. Their weapons, the modified hairs we call "quills," are formidable in appearance but purely defensive in function. A porcupine will drive its quills deep into the flesh of another animal only upon provocation.

Second, porcupine females are good mothers. After giving birth heroically and without assistance to a single thorny porcupette (which, by the way, weighs nearly twice as much as the newborn cub of a black bear), Mother Porcupine nurses her baby for three and a half months. (Dad, meanwhile, is presumably off hunting for tools, fishing poles, and parked cars.)

Third, porcupines enrich the English language. They have given us adjectives (*porcupinish* and *porcupiny*) and a verb (*to porcupine*, as in "When Albert inserted his finger into the electrical socket, his hair porcupined"), all three of which merit inclusion in the *Oxford English Dictionary*.

Finally (although more points could be driven home in a longer essay), porcupines are good to eat—if, that is, you can get beyond each individual's 30,000 quills. The American Indians ate porcupines. So today do cat-size weasels of the north woods, called fishers. For a hungry fisher to face the prickly situation of attacking a porcupine, guile and daring are required. The fisher must bite the porcupine on the head, where it has few quills, or on the belly, where it has none. Sometimes the fisher emerges victorious. But often the porcupine, happily conceding a few minor points, ambles into the undergrowth unharmed.

Any self-respecting porcupine would bristle at the suggestion (made by some writers) that members of his species are stupid and clumsy. True, porcupines are heavy of body, and their movements on the ground and in trees are less than graceful. But approach one, needle it with the end of a stick, and you will see the porcupine at his nimble menacing best. The naturalist John Burroughs once tried to catch a porcupine in a blanket. He succeeded, but not before collecting a handful of quills. These had to be plucked out, painfully, one by one. A lesson was learned: "The tail of a porcupine," Burroughs wrote, "goes with a spring like a trap. It seems to be a set-lock; and you no sooner touch with the weight of a hair one of the quills than the tail leaps up in a most surprising manner, and the laugh is not on your side."

Left to their own devices, porcupines, which are actually a species of rodent, devote the bulk of their time to eating and sleeping. Their food consists chiefly of the bark, buds, and twigs of hemlock, basswood, poplar, beech, birch, ash, oak, pine, spruce, and fir, although they also harbor passions for aquatic plants such as water lily and arrowhead. Porcupines sleep, not very neatly, in dens littered with their own droppings.

Viewed up close, the quills of a porcupine look like short knitting needles. Under magnification one can see that the tip of each bristles with tiny, backward-facing barbs. So effectively do these barbed quills defend their owners that, for any predator other than the fisher, attacking a porcupine is pretty much pointless.

7

Chipmunks: A Tribute

*I*n all the world, is there an animal more beautiful, more pleasing to the eye, than the common chipmunk of our backyards and woodlands? Admittedly, in a cosmopolitan zoological beauty contest, the chipmunk would have rivals. The lion, with its noble head and graceful gait, and the scarlet macaw, with its brilliant colors and broadsword tail, are thrilling to behold, and for sheer irresistibility no beast can out-cute the koala and the panda. But all things considered, the chipmunk, with its appealing nose, immaculate whiskers, well-proportioned face, cinnamon-colored pelage, and trademark black-and-white stripes, must be placed among the animal kingdom's standouts.

Chipmunks are generally underappreciated, except by children. They are small creatures, of course, and do not lend themselves to dramatic exhibits in zoos. (To my knowledge, no zoo, American or otherwise, has a chipmunk house.) Chipmunks are also squirrels, and as such tend to be lumped with their sibling species as pests. This is not entirely fair. Unlike gray squirrels, chipmunks rarely invade attics, chew insulation from power lines, or drive birdfeeding humans into bankruptcy. Generally they are easy creatures to get along with.

This is not to say that chipmunks are saints and gray squirrels are sinners. Gray squirrels have as much right to life, liberty, and the pursuit of happiness as any species, regardless of how humans may view their behavior, and chipmunks are anything but blameless. The critical difference is that when chipmunks exhibit the kinds of behavior that humans find objectionable, they do it discreetly, out of view.

For example, it is widely known that chipmunks eat nuts, seeds, and berries. In cheek pouches they carry these foods back to their dens, saving them for snacks and winter consumption. This all sounds cozy and innocuous, unless you are a parent plant trying to raise offspring. However, although few people are aware of it, chipmunks also hunger for flesh. Scientists have found that chipmunks, when not dining on vegetable matter, will subdue and devour such hearty fare as songbirds (slow-moving sparrows are a favorite), bird and amphibian eggs, nestling birds, moles, mice, snakes, frogs, salamanders, and butterflies. So it seems that the mild-mannered chipmunk is really not so mild mannered after all.

According to current scientific opinion, exactly twenty chipmunk species inhabit America north of the Rio Grande. Of these, only one, the eastern chipmunk, resides in the Northeast. The rest, including the alpine chipmunk of the Sierra Nevada and the gray-collared chipmunk of Arizona and New Mexico, inhabit the Far West. California, which has thirteen resident species, is the chipmunk capital of the world.

In the northern states, and in high-altitude habitats in the Southwest, chipmunks spend all or part of each winter underground. They retreat into their burrows, and snug within, they dine on the fruits and seeds they have spent the whole year gathering and storing. Unlike woodchucks, which swell to immense proportions as they put on autumn fat, chipmunks maintain their slender, pleasing proportions year-round.

For decades scientists have been attempting to determine whether or not chipmunks hibernate. (Hibernation, according to the experts, is more than a simple state of inactivity; it also involves a dramatic lowering of heart rate, respiration rate, and body temperature that bring the hibernating animal to the verge of death.) One researcher studying a population of eastern chipmunks found that 30 percent of the animals hibernated, 60 percent did not, and 10 percent couldn't make up their minds.

The implication? It seems that chipmunks, like people, are idiosyncratic.

The Beaver: Builder of Dams, Unexpected Houseguest

It would be hard to say which has a greater impact on the American landscape, the Army Corps of Engineers or the beaver. Both make placid reservoirs from rushing rivers. Both dig canals. Both are loved and hated, in about equal measure, by their neighbors. But upon close consideration, the beaver gets the edge. The Army Corps of Engineers has been in business only for a couple of centuries. The beaver has been at work since the Ice Age.

Beavers, like the men and women of the Army Corps, are tireless dam builders. Some of their dams are as impressive, in their rustic stick-and-mud way, as the great walls of reinforced concrete known as the Hoover and the Grand Coulee. By way of example, one beaver dam on the Jefferson River in Montana was measured by a biologist and found to stretch twenty-three hundred feet from end to end—nearly half a mile! Beaver dams can rise to heights of ten feet and more, and they can last for centuries.

To erect dams and to construct the artificial islands that serve them as lodges, beavers must be massive and powerful. They are; in fact, the beaver is the world's second largest rodent—only the capybara of South America is bigger. Although the average weight of an adult beaver is about thirty pounds, a few well-fed individuals have weighed twice that and more.

The strength of a beaver is exerted on both ends, the head and the tail. The head end of a beaver houses two sturdy jawbones, bones which in turn hold sharp incisor teeth that never stop growing. Thick muscles wrap around the beaver's rugged skull, and these power the incisors through almost anything a beaver fancies as food or lumber. The molar teeth of the beaver are broad and ridged.

The tail of a beaver is long (up to sixteen inches), wide (four inches or more), and fleshy. It is a powerful appendage that the beaver uses in water to propel itself and to maneuver. Beaver tails were long considered a delicacy in Europe. They were so much in demand among the clergy, in fact, that in 1754 a Paris Jesuit with flexible morals pronounced beaver tails "completely fish" so that their flesh could be enjoyed on Fridays.

Beavers, like humans, create their own habitats by directly altering the environment. Aquatic creatures, they dam streams and flood valleys to give them easy access to food, which for a beaver consists chiefly of aquatic plants such as the water lily and the bark of poplars, willows, and aspens. Water also provides safety for the slow, lumbering beaver from terrestrial predators such as wolves, coyotes, and foxes. Because it is dangerous for beavers to stray far from water, a family of beavers that depletes the supply of trees along the shores of its reservoir is briefly in trouble. The problem is easily surmounted, however, by adding sticks and mud to the beaver dam. Thus the water level rises and the pond expands into new feeding grounds where the beavers can operate in safety.

Also like humans, beavers are agents of drastic ecological change. Every time they flood a valley, beavers unwittingly displace terrestrial plants and animals while creating new habitats for aquatic species. Poplars, willows, and aspens, upon which the beaver feeds, and ruffed grouse, woodchucks, and box turtles, which prefer fairly dry conditions, are probably no fans of the beaver. On the other hand, creatures that thrive in wet conditions—turtles, frogs, salamanders, and water snakes, to cite a few examples—are undoubtedly the beaver's greatest admirers.

Humans, by and large, have mixed feelings about beavers. The funniest telephone call I ever received came from a woman who lived in North Salem, New York, near a swamp. One warm day when the front door of her house stood open to let in the air, a fully grown beaver marched up the woman's front steps and into her living room. It was there *now*, she told me quite emphatically. She didn't want to hurt the beaver, nor did she want the beaver to wreak havoc in her home. What should she do?

I am afraid that I lost my professional composure and laughed. Fortunately the woman with the beaver laughed too. She was good-humored and acknowledged that her question was extraordinary. After discussing several options for ejecting the uninvited houseguest, we decided in the end that the best thing for her to do was to approach the beaver cautiously and, with a broom, try to coax it out the door. Curious to know how the story would end, I asked the woman to telephone me after the beaver had gone. She never did. Years later I still find myself wondering about the outcome.

9

The Masked Shrew

M ammals, by and large, are big. An adult blue whale may stretch 110 feet from stem to stern, for example, and weigh as much as ninety tons. An African elephant may weigh six tons (more if his trunk is full) and a rhinoceros half that much. And the moose, the heftiest land mammal in the northeastern United States, can, if well fed and in antler, weigh a thousand pounds, give or take a few hundred.

How amazing, then, that the masked shrew, an abundant resident of woods and meadows across the northern United States and Canada, is kin to these behemoths. A masked shrew is only about four inches long, and nearly half of that is accounted for by a tail no thicker than pencil lead. A chubby masked shrew weighs about a fifth of an ounce, a slim one about a tenth. But make no mistake: the masked shrew is just as much a mammal as its biggest cousins. Even though comparable in size to a large bumblebee, the mother masked shrew suckles her offspring with milk of her own manufacture, just like her gargantuan relations.

As any short person will tell you, wonderful things come in small packages. To this rule the masked shrew is no exception. Masked shrews are daring climbers, capable swimmers, fierce hunters, and caring parents. They brim with energy—so much so that they might be considered the Teddy Roosevelts of the mammal world. The heart of a masked shrew beats about 1,200 times every minute.

One summer, I was able to learn a few things about masked shrews firsthand. My introduction to the animals came by accident. As part of a research project, I was trying to catch jumping mice. There are two species where I live, and because it is all but impossible to determine to which species a particular mouse belongs without examining it up close, I had set a dozen box traps in a meadow where the mice had been seen. As it happened I had no luck catching jumping mice. Plenty of rodents were collected, but all were white-footed mice. Not ready to give up, I replaced the box traps with pit traps. These were simply industrial-size mayonnaise jars given to me by Dan Delaney, a friend who worked in a local delicatessen. To turn the jars into traps, I buried them up to their necks in the meadow. No bait was necessary; the near-sighted mice would simply bumble into the openings and escape would be impossible.

Success came on the very first night, although not in subduing the intended quarry. In one of the jars I was surprised to find three shrews. They were tiny—the largest had a torso no thicker or longer than the outer joint of my thumb—and colored cinnamon brown. Gazing down at them, I felt a bit like Gulliver towering over the citizens of Lilliput. Two of the shrews were dead. Their little corpses were disfigured by gaping holes, around which some of the flesh had been eaten away.

The third shrew was the very picture of health. It circled around and around the base of the jar like a runner on a short track, wiggling a diminutive set of whiskers as it ran. This shrew was plump, and I suspected it had cannibalized its companions. Such behavior is not unusual among shrews, which have extraordinarily high metabolic rates and eat almost continually.

I was pretty sure the shrews were masked shrews, but to be certain I carried the two dead animals home in the breast pocket of my shirt so that I could examine their jawbones under a microscope. (Masked shrews, unfortunately, are maskless. Why they are so named I cannot say, save to remark that the scientists who name peculiar animals like shrews are often rather peculiar themselves.) The jawbones told me nothing, although not through any fault of their own. I was (and I remain) a dilettante in the business of examining shrew mandibula and couldn't make out the differences the books told me to look for. So I packaged the jawbones and shipped them, teeth and all, to the Department of Mammalogy at the American Museum of Natural History. There, I hoped, an expert could identify the specimens conclusively. About a year later, a reply arrived in the mail. The jawbones were, in fact, those of *Sorex cinereus*, the masked shrew, as I had suspected.

My experience when trapping masked shrews—finding one alive and two dead in a set of three—agrees with general scientific opinion. Alfred Godin, in *Wild Mammals of New England*, describes masked shrews as "restless, pugnacious, and voracious" and says that they will eat others of their kind. In bolstering these points he cites a 1932 study by Philip Bloom that found that one masked shrew, a captive, wolfed down more than three times its weight in food during each of the days it was observed. This shrew was obviously a glutton, but even if others are less rapacious, it is clear that masked shrews are big eaters and have no scruples about devouring their relations. From this it is a small leap to infer that young shrews probably lose trust in their parents at an early age.

You may never come upon a blue whale, an elephant, or a rhinoceros in the wild, unless you are especially lucky. But sprawl across the wet grass of a meadow at dawn and peer into a mayonnaise jar put out the night before, and you may find yourself eye-to-eye with a masked shrew. There, certainly, you may count yourself lucky.

10
Weasels: Bloodlust and Sucking Eggs

I can suck melancholy out of a song as a weasel sucks eggs.
—*William Shakespeare,* As You Like It

For centuries, humans have conscripted the long-tailed weasel and its American and European cousins and pressed them into service as symbols of greed, bloodlust, rapacity, and ugliness. Ernest Thompson Seton voiced the opinion of most naturalists in the early part of the present century when he said that weasels, as a group, are "bloodthirsty." Seton wrote: "No creature that lives is more thoroughly possessed of the lust for blood than the slim-bodied weasel. They hunt tirelessly, following their prey by scent, and kill for the mere joy of killing, often leaving their victims and hurrying on for more. . . ." At other times, according to Seton, weasels "content themselves with merely sucking the warm blood."

Several times a year I hear someone compare the face of an acquaintance to that of a weasel. Such remarks are intended as disparagement, or so I assume. Whatever the intent, it is difficult to determine whether human or weasel suffers the greater insult. Lions are more magnificent and gazelles more graceful, but to my eyes there are few mammals more handsome and elegantly put together than *Mustela frenata,* the common long-tailed weasel.

Weasels are long and lithe. Adult male long-tailed weasels average about fifteen inches in length, with furry tails trailing five or six inches behind them. Female weasels are smaller. An average adult female long-tailed weasel measures about a foot from nose to hindquarters and weighs a mere three or four ounces.

Weasels are rarely seen, but recently a colleague and I had the good fortune of watching a weasel for a minute or more. The sighting took place in a pine forest where red squirrels are commonly observed, so when a long, brown, bushy-tailed mammal streaked into view, running along the top of an old stone fence, I was ready to pronounce it a squirrel. As the words left my lips, however, the animal stopped and turned to face us, and I knew my identification was wrong.

There was no mistaking the slender, flexible, sausage-shape body, the tiny legs, the upturned ears, and the pert little face that sized us up with quiet concern. Then, apparently upon determining two humans not worthy of fear or investigation, the weasel hurried along its way. We watched it run, negotiating the ups and downs of the wall, crossing a wide trail, and vanishing into undergrowth on the far side of the path.

Identifying weasels in the field is a tricky business. Both long-tailed and short-tailed weasels inhabit the area where our sighting took place, and although the two species differ considerably in overall size and tail length, the differences are not so great that a fleeting glance—this is usually all one gets of a weasel—is likely to yield a reliable identification. Fortunately, the weasel my colleague and I saw remained in view long enough for us to estimate its body length at about sixteen inches, and to get several good looks at its long, well-furred tail. With reasonable certainty we declared it a long-tailed weasel.

The pelage of a wild, healthy, free-roaming weasel is striking. The hair is so fine and soft that it begs to be petted, although to attempt this, if one of the speedy animals were captured, would be to invite a painful bite. On the face, flanks, back, and tail, the long-tailed weasel's coat is colored a rich chestnut brown. Underneath and along the insides of the legs, the fur is a rich creamy white.

Each time I see a weasel I'm struck by the way the brown fur on the weasel's sides meets the white of the belly. The line where the colors meet is perfectly defined; there is nothing vague or gradual about it. Aesthetically, there's something wonderful and comical about the way the line runs the full length of the animal's body and flows and bends plastically with its movements. To my eyes, the soft, loose-fitting pelage of the weasel suggests a comfy, old-fashioned set of Dr. Denton's pajamas.

Weasels molt their fur in fall and spring. After the autumn molt the fur of many long-tailed weasels is as white as fresh-fallen snow, although some individuals in a given area usually remain brown. When spring comes the winter camouflage is shed. The weasel then grows a new brown summer coat to replace it.

Are weasels bloodthirsty? Mice might think so, but by human standards weasels are just efficient at doing what evolution designed them for: killing and devouring small animals with an immaculate set of thirty-four very sharp teeth. The notion that weasels suck the blood of their victims has been discarded by modern research. Weasels will sometimes lick briefly the blood of a victim's wounds, but soon enough they get down to business and consume a hearty meal of flesh and viscera. They *will* eat the contents of eggs, as Shakespeare noted, but their diet consists mainly of mice, voles, rats, shrews, rabbits, chipmunks, frogs, and snakes.

Weasels are for the most part solitary, and are perhaps rightly famed for not getting along with their neighbors. Breeding, therefore, is a rough-and-ready affair. A male induces ovulation in a female by grabbing her by the scruff of the neck and dragging her around. The male is larger and considerably more powerful, so a female thus treated has little choice but to submit. The actual mating, which takes place in summer, is prolonged and repeated. The following spring, four to eight young are born. There is some evidence suggesting that males help in feeding and defending the litter, although the exact extent of their contribution is uncertain.

Perhaps weasels are to be admired most for their tenacity. The naturalist and wildlife photographer Leonard Lee Rue III described an occasion when he came upon a weasel dragging a rabbit back to its den in a woodpile. Such a scene is a rare find for a photographer, so Rue was eager to photograph it. But he needed additional equipment to do the subject justice—equipment that was far away at his home. Rue, a supremely enterprising man, had an idea. He approached the weasel, which had no intention of relinquishing its hard-won meal, and while it continued to tug on the neck of its victim, he grabbed a leg of the rabbit and with a length of cord tied it to a nearby tree. When he returned some time later with the needed gear, Rue found the cord intact and the weasel still struggling to bring the rabbit to the woodpile. Elephants never forget, and weasels, it seems, never, ever surrender.

11
The Eastern Coyote: A New Dog in Town

*S*ometime soon, while putting out the trash on a moonlit evening or while driving home along a desolate stretch of road on a dark night, you may find yourself headlights-to-eye with a creature that looks amazingly like a wolf. Your first instinct, perhaps, will be to convince yourself that this is merely a neighbor's German shepherd, out for its bedtime jaunt. But something isn't quite right. There is something unusual about this "dog." Its snout is too pointed, its forequarters too robust, and the look in its eyes is wild and chilling. Now, if you are alone and have a vivid imagination, you may start to think of werewolves.

Werewolves, however, live only in Hollywood films; real wolves, which stalked the fringes of American cities in colonial times, were trapped, hunted, and poisoned into oblivion (except in remote tracts of wilderness) by the time "Roosevelt" was first painted on the White House mailbox. You can be reasonably certain, then, that you glimpsed not Lon Chaney, Jr., pasted liberally with pelage, nor *Canis lupus*, the timber wolf, but the wolf's compact cousin, *Canis latrans*, best known as the coyote.

There is some debate as to when the first coyotes appeared in the Northeast. Some scientists propose that coyotes always have inhabited the region but, until recently, were confused with wolves, which they closely resemble. On the other hand, the majority view holds that coyotes from the Midwest began colonizing the northeastern states early in the present century. Stanley Grierson, a widely respected naturalist who was active in New York's Westchester County suburbs from the 1930s through the 1960s, told me via telephone from his present home in Maine that coyotes first began appearing in Westchester County in the 1950s.

Until recently, scientists called the secretive wolflike animals the "northeastern wild canid." Studying specimens killed by cars, hunters, and trappers, they noted that these animals were not wolves, nor were they simply eastern versions of the western coyote. The wild canids of the East were nearly wolfish in stature, ranging from 50 to 75 percent heavier than western coyotes. Further, they had bigger nosepads, broader snouts, darker coats, and proportionately larger feet than the coyotes, say, of Texas or Nevada. And field observers, who listened at night to the eastern canids communicating with each other, claimed that they howled like wolves.

A controversy ensued. Some naturalists argued that the eastern canids *were* wolves. Others claimed that they were wild dogs or "coy-dogs"—crosses between domestic dogs and wild coyotes. A few authorities maintained that the problematic beasts were genuine coyotes, but of a new eastern variety. Eventually, researchers solved at least part of the mystery. At Harvard University, a statistical study of measurements taken from eastern canid skulls found significant differences between these skulls and those of wolves, dogs, and coy-dogs. And in New Hampshire, a captive breeding study showed the eastern wild canid's breeding pattern to be similar to that of western coyotes. Males and females mated only in late winter; when the pups were born in spring, the males assisted in rearing them. By contrast, coy-dogs, it was found, bred in fall and gave birth in the middle of the harsh New England winter, and, as with domestic dogs, the males provided no help to the females in raising the young. (Not surprisingly, in cold climates wild dogs and coy-dogs rarely survive more than a single generation in the wild.)

Yet, the eastern canids were not simply western coyotes transplanted. They were too big, too broad, too wolflike. Scientists began to wonder: could the eastern animals be coyote-wolf hybrids?

Early research tended to undermine this hypothesis. The New Hampshire breeding studies showed that the eastern canids bred true. (In other words, their puppies were generally uniform in size, shape, and color. Crosses between hybrids generally result in highly variable offspring.) And a dark shadow on the coyote-wolf hybridization theory was cast by field reports: when coyotes ventured into territories inhabited by wolves, observers found that the wolves destroyed the coyotes swiftly, apparently out of sheer antagonism. Behavioral dogma, therefore, insisted that coyotes and wolves never mixed.

Dogma's bark was at least partially silenced by the Harvard skull studies. Results not only showed significant similarities between the wild canid skulls and the skulls of coyotes but also suggested that somehow, somewhere, non-coyote genes might have spilled into the gene pool. Where did the genes come from? At present no one can say, but the most likely direction to point the proverbial finger is in the direction of the wolf.

Whatever their origin, coyotes have come to stay. If you live in the East and have not yet seen one, you may sometime soon. Sightings take place most often at dawn and dusk, frequently along roads. Like humans, coyotes are intelligent opportunists. Deer, raccoons, opossums, and other animals killed by speeding automobiles offer an abundance of food for the taking.

Western coyotes are inefficient predators of large animals such as deer. They feed mostly on rodents, rabbits, and birds—sheep ranchers' claims notwithstanding. The larger eastern coyotes, as we can now call them, are proving more successful in stalking big game. This is probably a good thing. Populations of whitetail deer in the East have reached such high levels that the native vegetation is suffering, and the deer themselves are being killed in appalling numbers on highways.

Let the coyotes have their fill of deer. If the ancient link between prey and predator is restored, the health of the deer herd will be improved, and perhaps some of the ferns and wildflowers that now vanish into the stomachs of underfed deer will return to their former abundance. And in eastern forests where the timber wolf has long been silent, let the song of the coyote, a mournful, haunting cacophony of yips and wails, carry far and resonate. If you listen you may hear one. The privilege will not be soon forgotten.

12

The Bobcat, A Feline
Abbreviated

*L*iving among us secretly, prowling the woods under cover of darkness, are wild, free-roaming cats as fierce as lions. They travel alone, patrolling several square miles of territory in a single night. Some hunt from trees and leap on unsuspecting deer that pass beneath. Others stalk their victims, creeping close on silent feet to foraging opossums and raccoons before making the final, fatal lunge. Some of the cats exploit the natural camouflage of their tawny, spotted fur and wait in a ready-to-spring crouch along trails followed habitually by deer and other animals. All the cats are well equipped by nature to satisfy their appetites.

If you happen to see one of these wild cats in a flashlight beam, or are lucky enough to get a look at one by daylight as it climbs a rocky slope, you will probably be startled. So will be the cat, which avoids human contact with greater success than other large wild animals. The cat that you see will stand about as high as a beagle. As it turns and vanishes, you will probably get a glimpse of its tail, which is unnaturally short. Now you can be certain that the abbreviated apparition was a bob-tailed cat, or simply, a bobcat.

If a bobcat was placed beside an ordinary house cat, the bobcat would appear substantially larger. On average, bobcats measure about thirty-eight inches end to end and stand about fifteen inches tall. Bobcats are also substantially heavier than their domesticated cousins and often weigh up to forty pounds. (A few enormous specimens weighing over fifty pounds have been recorded.) The coloring of a bobcat is reminiscent of that of a tabby house cat. The background color ranges from gray to red-brown. Streaks and spots are black. The short tail, about five or six inches long, is banded light and dark, and usually is marked by a white patch just on or behind the tip. The face of the bobcat is broad and encircled by a handsome, fluffy ruff.

A bobcat's eyes are large and yellow. They are located forward on the skull, like the eyes of humans and owls, giving the cats excellent binocular vision, which helps in gauging the distance of leaps from hidden positions onto the necks of unsuspecting victims. If you see a bobcat at night you will notice that its eyes shine brightly, as if radiating some inner malevolence. In fact, the back of each eye is lined with a reflective layer, known as the tapetum lucidum, which helps to intensify images seen in low light. The bobcat's eyes seem to glow because a portion of the light that enters the eyes is reflected back toward its source.

The most amazing thing about a bobcat is its strength. Owing to its small size (compared to mountain lions, jaguars, and other large cats, the bobcat is a pip-squeak), scientists long assumed that the bobcat fed mainly on small prey such as rabbits, mice, and birds. But recent research suggests that bobcats feed regularly on adult deer.

With powerful legs that can carry them six or eight feet in a single bound, bobcats leap onto passing bucks and does. If all goes well for the bobcat, it lands on the deer's neck, and there with its sharp teeth it severs the jugular vein. A downed deer provides a feast for a lone cat. What cannot be eaten at one meal is buried, or partially buried. The bobcat will return and continue to feed until the meat begins to spoil. Solitary creatures, bobcats do not share their kills without a fight.

Late in the winter, bobcat males and females, separate for most of the year, seek each other out for breeding. Courtship is handled carefully. The cats, which at best are wary and at worst are combative around others of their kind, must negotiate a truce before a romance can be pursued. A sensitive area in the roof of the mouth called a Jacobson's organ probably helps bobcats to detect, through airborne scents and pheromones, the sex and intentions of their prospective mates.

During the January and February mating, humans are most likely to learn of the presence of bobcats. Breeding can be a noisy affair. The sound of bobcat cries late at night in a dark forest are bone chilling and not easily ignored.

After a gestation of about sixty-two days, bobcat kittens (usually in a litter of three) are born in their mother's den. Dens are often located in rocky cliffs where crevices provide safe, dry shelter. Hollow trees and logs are also used. The kittens are born blind, their bright blue eyes opening in about ten days. Weaning begins at about eight weeks, a time when the blue of the kittens' eyes begins to fade to the yellow of adult eyes. Most of the young cats are on their own by late autumn. Many, unable to catch enough mice, rabbits, mink, shrews, moles, chipmunks, and birds to fulfill their energy needs, die. A few young cats are caught and consumed by owls, foxes, and coyotes.

A young bobcat that survives the first challenging months of its independence will grow up to lead a wandering, solitary life. Through the deep snows of midwinter nights, under the orange moons of steamy August dawns, and through all the nights of the long year, the bobcat will prowl. Only its tracks, large like a dog's but lacking claw marks, will betray the bobcat's activities and whereabouts, unless a perceptive hiker finds a buried deer carcass with a torn neck or a rank-smelling den and knows how to interpret the discovery.

The bobcat's secret life allows it to persist on the edges of civilization where more conspicuous predators such as the timber wolf and the panther were exterminated long ago. Wary and camouflaged, it thrives in our country woodlots and wooded suburbs, living as invisibly as an owl, hunting with the ferocity of a lion.

13

Armadillos: Mammals in Armor

To gaze upon an armadillo, as I did during a recent visit to Florida, is to test your credulity. The experts call this armor-plated, primitive, lumbering creature a mammal. Yet look at an armadillo, and you will see that it lacks body hair and is covered with scales. The question arises: why not call it a reptile?

Believe it or not, and despite appearances, the reasons for considering armadillos mammals are compelling. First, the armadillo maintains a fairly steady body temperature. Granted, the thermostat is set low—an armadillo never gets warmer inside than about ninety-six degrees Fahrenheit—but it is a thermostat nonetheless, and the setting holds pretty much constant. Second, a mother armadillo nourishes her young (these are born in identical sets of four) with milk of her own manufacture. Third, an armadillo is covered with hair. Hair? Admittedly one has to look carefully to see it.

Not long ago, on Cumberland Island off the coast of Georgia, I had an opportunity to observe armadillos at close range. Armadillos are newcomers to Cumberland's forests of live oak and palmetto. National Park Service scientists estimate that armadillos first arrived on the island around 1974, and in its relative tranquillity, the armored mammals have thrived. A bonus for naturalists and wildlife watchers is that the Cumberland armadillos are nearly fearless and can be approached at any time of the day. Elsewhere, armadillos are active mostly at night.

Near Dungeness, the crumbled ruin of a mansion built on Cumberland Island by Thomas and Lucy Carnegie in the 1880s, I got my first close look at an armadillo on a sunny autumn afternoon. Three of the animals were snuffling to and fro across an open lawn, and when I approached, they paid no attention to me. I noticed at once that the armadillos indeed had hair. On the back of each animal, the hard bony plates (the armadillo's trademark) were covered with fuzz of the sort that covers a peach. And on the belly and throat, each armadillo was shaggy with hairs that were coarse, gray, and dirty. Armadillos in illustrations tend to appear tidy and clean, but real armadillos spend their lives on the ground, digging in the soil. I learned on Cumberland Island that the typical armadillo appears in desperate need of a bath.

When feeding, an armadillo sniffs and shuffles along the ground, seeking the aroma of insects in the soil. The sense of smell in an armadillo is keen. When it has found what it is sniffing for, an armadillo digs furiously with its front feet. The feet are clawed, and they make short work of rooting out grubs and ants. These morsels the armadillo swallows hungrily, chewing with simple, rootless teeth.

The nine-banded armadillo of Cumberland Island and much of the American South is the only species of armadillo that lives north of Mexico. Overall, however, there are twenty species. The others live in Central and South America. Armadillos are edentates, meaning that they are close relations of anteaters, sloths, and pangolins. The scientific name of the nine-banded armadillo is *Dasypus novemcinctus*, which when spoken out loud sounds like a Gregorian chant.

14

Pronghorn of the Prairies: At Home on the Range

The strangest mammal in North America is not the porcupine, which bears quills, or the opossum, which carries its dependents in a pouch, but the antelopelike creature of the Western plains we call the pronghorn. The pronghorn is not a deer, although in form and size it resembles a deer, and it is not an antelope, despite the fact that naturalists sometimes slip and call it one. In truth, the pronghorn is simply a pronghorn—the lone survivor of a family of hooved animals that evolved in North America, thrived here for eons, and then, with a lone exception, vanished.

Among our hooved animals, the pronghorn is the patriarch. When the ancestors of the moose, deer, elk, caribou, and bison that inhabit North America today crossed from their Asian homeland to Alaska on a land bridge, they arrived in a place that had already been long inhabited by pronghorn. Pronghorn have been at home on the ranges of the American West for more than a million years. Ironically, they are probably the least known of our ungulates. I find that some easterners have never heard of pronghorn, and those that have often assume that pronghorn are exotic creatures that must have escaped from zoos.

Why the pronghorn survived while all its near kin died out no one can say. Perhaps it was simply a matter of speed. Among the most fleet-footed animals on earth, the pronghorn can run fifty miles per hour, far faster than the wolves, coyotes, and cougars that hunt it. Bounding across the prairie at full-tilt, the stride of a pronghorn may measure an astounding twenty-seven feet.

"So rapidly do their legs perform their graceful movements in propelling their bodies over the ground," John James Audubon wrote of the pronghorn, "that like the spokes of a fast-turning wheel we can hardly see them, but instead, observe a gauzy or film-like appearance where they should be visible." I well remember my own first sighting of pronghorn along a highway in Texas. One moment about a dozen of the graceful tan and white animals were beside the car, and the next moment they were gone. By stepping between the strands of a wire fence and bounding away toward the horizon, the pronghorn vanished like smoke in the wind.

In addition to being fast, pronghorn are wary. Their wide black eyes bulge out from the sides of their heads like fish-eye lenses, and these give the animals a peripheral vision that takes in a complete 360-degree sweep. Approaching a pronghorn on the Western plains is virtually impossible. Typically, the animal will spot your movement before you can get within miles of it. Indian hunters, it is said, lured pronghorn within spear-and-arrow range by lying on their backs and kicking their feet in the air. The pronghorn, which are innately curious, came close and the Indians killed them. Later, European pioneers modified the trick, waving handkerchiefs on the ends of sticks or ramrods. These ploys worked all too well, and by 1900 it is estimated that pronghorn numbers had dropped from at least 40 million a century earlier to a low of about 19,000.

During the twentieth century, pronghorn numbers have rebounded. Today scientists estimate that more than 450,000 inhabit prairies and brushlands from southern Saskatchewan, Montana, Idaho, and the Dakotas south to Texas, New Mexico, Arizona, and northern portions of Mexico.

The pronghorn is unique in that, despite the permanence of its horns, the horns' outer sheaths are shed and regrown yearly like antlers. (Generally, horns are permanent and antlers are temporary, but the pronghorn muddies this distinction.) The sheaths of pronghorn horns are made of keratin. If you hold one in your hand and examine it closely, you will see that, like a rhinoceros horn, it is made up of hairs that are fused tightly. The horns themselves are black in color. They measure three or four inches on the doe and grow up to twenty inches on the buck. The doe's horns are straight and unbranched, but jutting forward on the buck's horns are sturdy projections, one on each. These "prongs" give the pronghorn, the most idiosyncratic of American mammals, its name.

15

Whitetail Deer: The Buck Stops Here

Hike into the woods on a clear, crisp November day. Listen to the rustle of dry leaves underfoot, and hear the chattering of black-capped chickadees in the treetops. You will soon come upon a small tree that catches your eye because a swath of bark has been violently scraped from its trunk. The wound is fresh, and if the day is warm, sap may ooze. Nearby is a spot where the fallen leaves have been pushed aside and the earth is scraped as if by an iron rake. If you are schooled in the ways of wildlife, you will know that these signs can mean only one thing: *the buck stops here.*

To be explicit, you have unwittingly discovered the trysting place of a male whitetail deer. For the buck, this place of bruised bark and tortured earth is the cervine equivalent of the human bachelor pad and waterbed, a spot where the female of the species, it is hoped, will stop and linger.

For deer, autumn is the season of courtship. Bucks become interested in the does long before the feelings are reciprocated. By the time the maples turn color, amorous bucks are seeking to consummate their desires with any living thing that moves. Does, fawns, and even younger bucks are fair game. As the time of actual breeding approaches—scientists call this the *rut*—the bucks begin to act in strange ways. They patrol territories. They scrape the earth. They urinate on their own hind legs, passing their excretions over scent glands that will leave the females lurid messages. Does come into heat only for a short period of time. Most of them come into season in autumn, generally around the middle of November. A few younger females, however, may withhold their favors until February or March.

During the waiting period, the bucks keep busy. As suitors, they are anything but patient. Does are pursued relentlessly day and night, hounded through thickets and swamps and followed across meadows and highways. To vent their frustrations, to fortify themselves for upcoming struggles with competing suitors, and perhaps also to keep themselves trim and muscular in the eyes of the womenfolk, the bucks work out on their version of the Nautilus machine. It consists of a set of saplings and small trees. Against these the bucks shove and grunt, scraping against the bark with their heads and antlers. In the process, the last tatters of summer velvet fall from the bucks' antlers, and their necks and torsos swell like a bodybuilder's. A prime buck in breeding season is the Arnold Schwarzenegger of the animal world.

As the buck paces his territory, he indulges in an activity that strikes humans as especially curious. One patch here, one patch there, he paws at the ground, scraping it bare. Then he urinates in the spot, hoping that the strong, musky-smelling odor of his excretion will warm the heart of a neighboring doe.

Bucks also meet for an occasional bout of serious, and only occasionally violent, sparring. In rare situations these struggles may be fatal; hikers sometimes find pairs of deer skulls locked together at the antlers. Such grim souvenirs are created when fighting bucks become entangled, and the gladiators, unable to retreat and refresh themselves, die slow deaths of starvation and exposure.

If a buck is lucky—for the most part, only the strongest, dominant males manage to breed—a doe, guided by her sensitive nose, will visit one of his bare, musky patches of earth. Here, if impressed by what she finds, she will sprinkle a bit of her own perfume, twitch her nose, blink her brown eyes, and wiggle her long ears. Somewhere nearby, the buck is ready.

Early some November morning while you are still asleep, the buck and the receptive doe will honor a family tradition that will perpetuate their bloodlines. If all goes well, they will remain together for a while, perhaps for two days or as long as two weeks. During this period of togetherness mating is the chief thing on their minds, and feeding and sleeping are reduced to a minimum.

Among whitetail deer monogamy is an unknown virtue. When the buck and doe part company, the buck goes back to his scrapes and resumes the search for other females. He will mate with as many does as he can in the days and weeks ahead. If he is the dominant male in his neck of the woods, the buck will likely meet with much success. Only the spring of a bobcat or a hunter's bullet can still his urges.

PART THREE

In Cold Blood

1
Horseshoe Crabs:
Crabs That Aren't

As a child, I was frightened by horseshoe crabs. As an adult, I am fascinated by them. The fear vanished when I learned that horseshoe crabs have no mouths with which to bite and no claws with which to pinch; they are, in fact, not really crabs at all.

Horseshoe crabs are not closely related to anyone or anything. They are not crabs and they are not spiders, but are placed in a zoological cubbyhole all their own. To look at a horseshoe crab is to gaze at a creature that has existed on earth almost since the beginning of time. Because they are so ancient and so unlike other creatures, horseshoe crabs fascinate everyone. Young children are intrigued by their tails and must either touch them or run away screaming. Teenagers find horseshoe crabs appealing because their bodies remind them of racing cars or flying saucers. Most adults are attracted to horseshoe crabs because they have seen them all their lives but somehow managed to learn almost nothing about them.

As an adult, I fall into the last-mentioned category. I have learned more in the last few weeks about horseshoe crabs than I had learned in the preceding three-and-a-half decades. No great event occurred to stimulate my sudden interest. I was simply gazing into a "touch tank" at a public aquarium in Biloxi, Mississippi, and there they were. I'd seen horseshoe crabs a hundred times before, but this time, a couple of nerve endings in my brain that had previously avoided each other suddenly connected, and I spent much of the ensuing week trying to learn about them what I could.

Horseshoe crabs, I discovered by rummaging through a zoology book, have blue blood, and not merely in a figurative sense. The oxygen-carrying agent in horseshoe crab blood is a copper-based compound, and because oxidized copper is blue, the crab's blood is blue. In humans, oxygen is carried by an iron-based compound called hemoglobin, and because the oxidized iron (or rust) in hemoglobin is red in color, human blood is red. (Contrary to popular belief, human blood is never blue, even when it flows through veins. It is bright red when oxygenated and dark red when returning to the lungs for a breath of fresh air.)

Another odd thing about horseshoe crabs is that they chew and swallow small, bottom-dwelling ocean creatures, even though they lack mouths capable of chewing. A conundrum, to be sure, but horseshoe crabs get around it by masticating their food not with their mouths but with their armpits. It works like this. Where the front legs of the horseshoe crab meet under the center of the shell, two opposing plates of bristles push against each other every time the animal takes a step. Hidden behind these plates is the entrance to the alimentary canal, a portal otherwise known as the mouth. As the horseshoe crab passes over wet sand, it cruises like a hovercraft over a variety of edible animals. The animals are caught by the bristles, bruised, and mashed for a while between the armpits, then drawn into the crab's waiting maw.

Horseshoe crabs have four eyes. The two obvious ones are located port and starboard on the front of the animal's shell and help it to muddle along through the sea and surf. The other eyes are positioned front and center on the shell and are thought to aid the crab in navigating long distances at sea.

Like other arthropods, horseshoe crabs shed their shells or exoskeletons as they grow. Examine a "dead" horseshoe crab carefully and you may find that it is not a complete animal at all but merely a carapace that has become too small for its owner.

At the end of a horseshoe crab is a long pointed tail. Until recently, I was among the many people not quite certain

whether this tail could or could not harm me. I gained illumi-
nation when a young man at the Biloxi aquarium put a live
horseshoe crab in my hand and, seeing my look of horror,
assured me that it could do no damage. I learned (and am glad
to report) that the tail of a horseshoe crab helps the animal to
propel itself through water and to right itself when overturned.
There is no venomous barb on it, as there is on the tail of a
stingray.

To sum up, the horseshoe crab, despite its ability to strike
terror into the hearts of five-year-olds, is perfectly harmless and
wonderfully interesting.

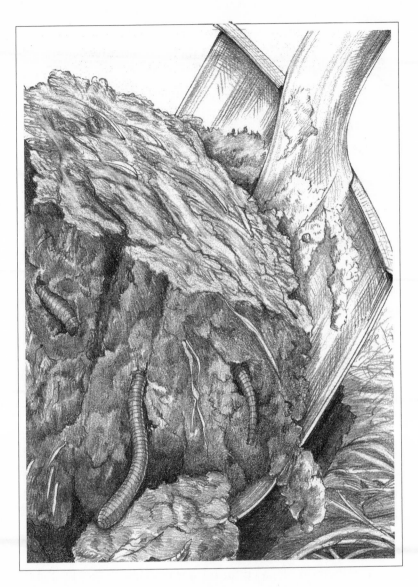

2

Earthworms and Charles Darwin: The Night Crawlers

Regarding the earthworm, Charles Darwin wrote, "It may be doubted there are many other animals which have played so important a part in the history of the world. . . ." Darwin wasn't joking. Nor was he writing of the bizarre giant earthworm, *Megascolides gippslandicus*, an Australian annelid that can grow as thick as a rake handle and up to ten feet in length, and which is located, according to the zoologist Allan Keast, by its "weird gurgling and bubbling sounds." In fact, Darwin referred to *Lumbricus terrestris*, the diminutive, humble, ever-so-common earthworm of England, Europe, and America.

Darwin's esteem for the earthworm arose from a lifetime of study. As a young man, before he sailed away on the *Beagle* and hatched the theory of evolution, Darwin became fascinated by earthworms. The interest never abated. As an old man, renowned in scientific and intellectual circles the world over, Darwin was often to be found in his garden, scrutinizing worm burrows and castings. His last published work was not a weighty tome on evolutionary theory but a book titled *The Formation of Vegetable Mould Through the Action of Worms*.

Why worms? One day in his garden Darwin noticed that a flagstone path he had not swept for several years had vanished. Probing the soil, he found the flagstones in perfect position, just where he had left them. They were buried, he observed, under more than an inch of loose, granular soil—a soil that seemed to consist almost entirely of worm droppings. This striking discovery inspired Darwin to raise earthworms in pots; to study them in his lawn, in his garden, and in nearby fields; and to collect the findings of fellow scientists who were similarly, terrestrially engaged. The results, as collected in his book on worms, are fascinating.

Did you know that a single acre of soil may teem with more than 50,000 worms? Collect them all (American robins and other worm-eating birds take note) and the worms would weigh nearly 400 pounds. Regarding the flagstones buried by worms in Darwin's garden, it seems that the carrying of soil to the surface by earthworms is a steady job. Worms egest partially digested materials, as all animals do, thus contributing to soil formation; and while burrowing through densely packed soil, they take dirt in through their mouths and pass it out through their rears. Much of this material is brought up to the surface, and objects lying on the ground, such as flagstones, get covered.

Earthworms, the white-haired naturalist tells us with boyish enthusiasm, may carry in a year to the surface of a single acre more than eighty tons of soil. He writes: "The plough is one of the most ancient and most valuable of man's inventions; but long before he existed the land was in fact regularly ploughed by earthworms." Darwin notes also that earthworms, although terrestrial creatures, are little changed from ancestors that lived in water. He reports the work of a French colleague, named Perrier, who found that while earthworms die if left exposed to the air for a single night, they can survive up to four months submerged in water. (Whether Perrier's water was naturally carbonated or not Darwin fails to explain.)

3

Ant Lions: Catchers
in the Rye

f you live where the soil is sandy, you may be harboring, in a dry corner of your lawn where the rye grass is patchy, a fierce predator called an ant lion. An ant lion is neither an antlike lion nor a leonine ant, but an insect of the order Neuroptera. Neuropterans are so-named because, in the adult stage, they possess wings crisscrossed by fine, nervelike veins. Only fully developed ant lions can fly, and then not very well.

As adults, ant lions eat little if at all. As larvae, they are voracious. Ant lions pass through a long adolescence for an insect—they exist in the larval stage of development for two or three years—and during this time, as with adolescents of our own species, there seems to be no end to their appetites. Cravings notwithstanding, ant lions do not possess stomachs that are bottomless pits. In fact, the digestive tract of a larval ant lion is literally a dead end. Solid materials that the ant lion does not digest can't be excreted and thus, by default, accumulate in the abdomen. Here they remain, carried like ballast for the rest of the insect's life. It is little wonder that adult ant lions are weak fliers.

By human standards, an ant lion larva is arguably the ugliest creature alive. Its most conspicuous features are sickle-shape mandibles, or jaws. These measure as much as a third the length of the larva's body, and they give the ant lion the look of a grim reaper with dual matching scythes. The body of the larva is shaped something like a bulldog's. It is short, squat, and muscular, designed by evolution to hold on, dig in, and not let go. From front end to tailgate there bristle coarse dark spines and out of the body sprout six stubby legs.

If you were an ant, you would not want to meet an ant lion. In fact, no small terrestrial creature would desire a meeting with an ant lion. One recent study examined 212 ant lion victims and found that only slightly more than a third of them were ants. The rest were a smorgasbord of terrestrial invertebrates—spiders, millipedes, sow bugs, and others. To catch prey, an ant lion uses its hind legs (these are modified for digging) to excavate a pit in the soil. The pit measures an inch or more across the top and just as deep, and it tapers toward the bottom like an ice cream cone buried point down in the soil. At the bottom, the ant lion buries itself, leaving only its jaws exposed. There it waits. Every ant lion is very patient. Instinctively it knows that sooner or later, some ant or other small arthropod will blunder into its trap.

When the moment comes, the ant lion is ready. It flicks grains of sand into the air, creating a landslide. As the walls of the pit give way, the victim struggles, but inevitably it tumbles downward. Soon the ant lion holds a meal in its maw.

Ant lions feed something like spiders. Through their mandibles, which are hollow like syringes, they inject a liquid into their prey that acts both as a poison and as a digestant. The ant lion grips its victim until this substance has had a chance to work. Then, perhaps with some sort of primitive satisfaction, it sucks up a liquid meal like a child drinking through a straw.

What to do with the victim's dry and lifeless carcass? With cool efficiency the ant lion solves this solid waste problem by flinging the corpse out of the pit. Now the catcher in the rye is ready to contemplate its next meal.

4

Beetles: The Insect Kingdom's Greatest Hits

Beatle stands between five foot eight and five
eleven and wears his hair in a style once described as "long." His face is distinguished by
two eyes, a single nose, and a mouth that sings.

A beetle is a six-legged arthropod, a member
of the class of invertebrates known as the insects. It has two
pairs of wings, the forward set of which function, when the
beetle is at rest, as protective covers for the rear pair, which are
thin and membranous. Beetles belong to the insect order
Coleoptera, meaning "sheath wing."

There are, or were, four known varieties of Beatle, all native
to Liverpool, in England. Tragically, the most colorful member
of the group is now extinct. The three survivors are rarely
sighted yet often heard.

There are, on earth, nearly 300,000 different kinds of beetles. At least that's how many we know of; undoubtedly, in the
tropics especially, there are thousands (perhaps hundreds of
thousands) waiting to be described. Only a paltry 30,000
species inhabit North America.

The Beatles are widely considered the most successful and
influential interpreters of that peculiar musical idiom known
as rock and roll. Although the group dispersed twenty years
ago, their music is still heard on every continent, including
Antarctica.

The beetles have also done well for themselves. They are
found here, there, and everywhere, in every conceivable habitat, from strawberry fields to Brazilian rain forest, from Kansas
City to Cape Town, from Penny Lane to the Boulevard
St.-Michel. In fact, among all the thousands of kinds of animals
on earth, one out of three is a beetle.

Many of our most familiar insects are beetles, even though
we may not recognize them as such. For example, fireflies are

not flies nor, despite their reputation as "lightning bugs," do they belong to that order of insects (the Hemiptera) that includes the so-called true bugs. Fireflies are beetles. Black and slender, they look like run-of-the-mill members of their clan by day. Only at night do they part wing covers and flash.

Water pennies, which live in cool streams and look like copper coins glued to the undersides of rocks, are beetle larvae. They feed on microscopic plants and animals and eventually, after metamorphosing into conventional-looking adults, take up residence on land.

June bugs are beetles. These are the insects whose carcasses have a way of turning up under porch lights and on windowsills by the bucketful. A typical adult June bug is about an inch long, with shiny brown wing covers. It feeds on the leaves of trees and, if a female, lays its eggs in soil. The eggs hatch, out crawl little grubs, and eventually (in two or three years) the grubs grow up to be June bugs.

Engraver beetles, burrowing in wood under the bark of trees, produce beautiful designs that resemble the famous drawings in the Peruvian desert at Nazca. Click beetles click. Predacious diving beetles dive, and wood-boring beetles, even as I write, are boring.

In sum, beetles rule the world and they are interesting. Next time you find one on the carpet, consider not squashing it.

Let it be.

5

Madame Butterfly

As she dances, she seems to float through the air with the grace of a butterfly. Why not? She *is* a butterfly, an aviatrix, if you will, of insectdom's most celebrated airborne division.

Madame Butterfly, like Monsieur, has a shapely three-parted body. Her first part is a head, her second a thorax, her third an ample abdomen. Upon the precious metallic head of Madame Butterfly are mounted two lovely compound eyes. Each of these consists of dozens of individual light-sensitive organs called ommatidia. Compound eyes provide compound images; therefore, each Monsieur that Madame looks upon is multifaceted. Madame Butterfly also possesses slender antennae, one above each of her eyes. At the end of each antenna is a tuft of fuzz, a sort of dislocated eyebrow.

If Madame sucks nectar (not all butterflies do), she will also possess a facial feature that, if female insects were vain, she might prefer that we ignore. I speak of a long proboscis. Such an organ is not attractive, except perhaps to a Monsieur with a long proboscis of his own, but there is no denying its usefulness. Coaxing nectar from a wildflower is hard work. Nectar is typically found deep in a blossom, and it takes a tool like a soda straw to draw it out.

Now we come to the thorax. Ah, the thorax: here Madame displays her second most conspicuous physical attribute, her powerful wing muscles. These attach to her first most conspicuous physical attribute, two pairs of broad expansive wings. Such wings! Poets write of them and Monsieur Butterfly (it can be presumed) delights in them. Madame's wings are usually bigger than her mate's. Typically, they display striking colors and patterns, the better to attract Messieurs with, and they may also aid in scaring away predators, blending in with backgrounds, and in helping Madame pass herself off as an inedible or poisonous look-alike. Madame's wings may also possess eye-spots or swallowtails. According to scientists, such embellishments probably succeed in deflecting the attention of hungry birds away from Madame's delicate vitals.

One thing about Madame Butterfly that cannot be denied—she has magnificent legs. Six of them.

Our anatomical survey now brings us to that most rounded and shapely third of a female butterfly, her abdomen. Madame's abdomen includes all the usual attributes of a distaff sexual animal: ovaries (hers called *ovarioles*), an oviduct, and a reservoir of eponymous purpose known as the *receptaculum seminis*. These are important parts. In the grand scheme of things, Madame's chief destiny (her *only* destiny in certain sybaritic species) is the mothering of offspring.

Mothering, for Madame, consists of nothing more or less than jettisoning eggs on the proper plants. In most species Madame does not need to concern herself with finding a mate. Monsieur finds her. He does so by sight and by fragrance. She radiates a heady perfume, and he possesses olfactory organs on his antennae so sensitive that he can detect her bouquet at great distances. Courtship, a rough-and-ready affair, is never operatic. Monsieur approaches. He gives off a pheremonal cologne of his own that, if he is lucky, Madame appreciates. (On male monarch butterflies, for example, the glands that produce this scent appear as black spots, one on each hind wing.) Whatever the effect, Monsieur Butterfly tries to coerce Madame into landing.

If he is successful, the determined Monsieur (who, let the truth be told, is more Rambo than Romeo) makes his decisive move. And Madame, if she is receptive, will commune with him—perhaps once, perhaps several times. Often, however, the lady is anything but willing. When she is not receptive,

Madame indicates disinterest in one of several ways—by waving her wings, by thrusting her abdomen indignantly in the air, or by flying off. Sometimes Monsieur takes the hint. Sometimes he does not.

Whatever action Madame takes, we may be certain that her course is honorable. (Honorable, that is, as much as honor can be defined in the colorful, premoral world of the butterfly.) It is a pity that certain species of her clan are branded with scarlet epithets such as "hoary comma" and "question mark." Better treatment is deserved, I think, and a few lucky Mesdames—"the monarch" and "the queen" come to mind—have managed to get it.

Cosmopolitan Butterflies: The Painted Ladies

Theirs is a universal profession. In Europe, in Asia, in Africa, throughout North and Central America, and in distant Australia and New Zealand, butterflies known as painted ladies ply a hoary trade: selling pollination services for nectar.

Known to lepidopterists as *Vanessa cardui*, the painted lady is the world's most widely distributed butterfly. It is a handsome creature, an animal whose appearance has no trouble fulfilling the promise of its name. The delicate upper surfaces of the painted lady's wings are colored a pastel salmon-orange, and upon these surfaces appear an array of spots: black spots over most of the wing area, and white spots toward the tips of the forewings. The wingspan of a painted lady, from forewing to forewing, measures from two to two-and-a-half inches.

Frequently, painted ladies are observed perched on flowers. At such times their wings are folded behind their backs, and the under, rather than the upper, sides of the wings are exposed. Here a series of small dark spots are visible near the hind wings' trailing edges. These are identifying features of *Vanessa cardui* and help to separate her from her look-alike relation, the American painted lady, *Vanessa virginiensis*. When you see a painted lady, perhaps in a red flower district on the other side of the railroad tracks, the best way to determine which species you are seeing is to ignore all other enticements and examine the undersides of the butterfly's hind wings. If several small dark spots parallel the trailing edges, you will know that the butterfly is a painted lady. If the hind wings are marked with two large blue spots, each ringed in black, you are gazing upon the painted lady's American cousin, *Vanessa virginiensis*.

The painted ladies that appear in summer across North America winter south of the Mexican border. On the opposite side of the Atlantic, painted ladies summer as far north as

Sweden and Norway and winter in the northern countries of Africa. In springtime, painted ladies throughout the Northern Hemisphere push northward in vast concentrations, making themselves abundant in some locales, scarce or nonexistent in others. Painted ladies are like solar eclipses; some years you see them, others you don't. One notable flight of these butterflies passed continuously over an observation point for three days. The painted ladies formed a front forty miles wide and they must have made a glorious sight. At times painted ladies are high fliers. A cloud of them was once recorded passing over Pakistan at an altitude of 17,000 feet.

If you'd like to see a painted lady, there is no need to venture into a shady side of town, or to fly to Tripoli or Stockholm. In summer, wade through any local meadow, old field, or vacant lot. Search for thistles, asters, ironweed, and joe-pye weed. These are colorful wildflowers that are not easily missed. Upon them you will likely find orange butterflies collecting nectar. Look closely. Some of the butterflies, if the year is a good one and conditions are right, may be painted ladies.

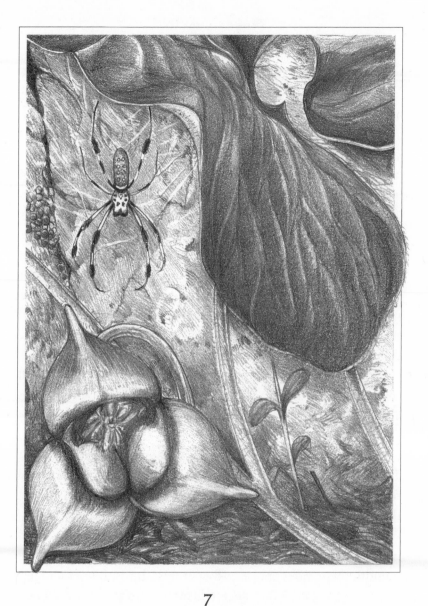

Spiders: Miss Muffet's Neighbors

Insects are insects and spiders are spiders, at least for the most part. An insect has three distinct body parts: a head, a thorax, and a plump abdomen. It also has six legs, one or two pairs of wings (these may or may not function), and antennae. A spider, by contrast, has only two body parts: a head fused to a thorax, together called a cephalothorax, and an abdomen. A spider also has two more legs than an insect (eight altogether, unless the spider has run into bad luck or an inquisitive child), and it lacks wings and antennae. Scientists who devote their lives to studying creeping, crawling things place insects in the class Insecta, spiders in the class Arachnida.

Spiders are found just about everywhere—in sun-scorched deserts, in dark forests, in even darker caves, on glaciers, under kitchen counters, in posh condominiums, in cool cellars, and snuggled among the chocolate chips inside cookie jars. In all the world there are 35,000 kinds of spiders, give or take a few thousand. Of these, about 3,000 inhabit North America.

It may or may not be comforting to know that although all spiders are venomous, the poisons produced by most species are lethal only to small creatures such as insects. Spiders subdue animals they fancy as food by biting them, then pumping venom into the resulting wounds through their mouthparts. The venom paralyzes the victim and liquefies its internal organs. Once the venom has done its work, the spider sucks out the unfortunate animal's insides.

Because spiders tend to be small, and because there are so many kinds of them, it is difficult for anyone but an expert to identify the various species. (By contrast, birds, bigger and less diversified, are easy for educated amateurs to sort out.) Do not, however, make the mistake of thinking that once you've seen one spider, you've seen them all.

Trapdoor spiders live in holes in the ground. They cover

the entrances to these holes with silken lids, and when insects step upon the lids, the spiders jump out and grab them. Comb-footed spiders, aside from being particularly well groomed, have structures on their feet that resemble hair combs. The most famous comb-footed spider is the black widow. (Note to the reader: do not feel sorry for the black widow. She is a widow because she ate her husband.)

Violin spiders have violin-shaped patterns on their backs. Never fiddle with them—several species manufacture dangerous venoms. Newly hatched spitting spiders, like all young spiders, are the spitting images of their parents. Spitting spiders don't need webs to catch their food. When a prospective meal walks by, the spider simply spits on it, and the sticky fluid immobilizes the prey long enough for the spider to capture it. Jumping spiders jump. Proving the wisdom of the old saying that it is important to look before you leap, jumping spiders have evolved bigger eyes and better long-distance vision than other spiders. Look at one closely and you may think it is wearing several pairs of sunglasses.

There are many other kinds of spiders: crab spiders, wolf spiders, orb weaving spiders, funnel web spiders, nursery web spiders, wandering spiders, and tarantulas. Ironically, the spider we most often see, the daddy long-legs, is not a spider at all.

Daddy long-legs differ from the so-called true spiders in several particulars. The cephalothorax and abdomen of the daddy long-legs are fused into a one-part torso; one cannot tell where the cephalothorax ends and the belly begins. The daddy long-legs also has two eyes, whereas most spiders have eight. Perhaps the greatest difference between the two arachnids involves the equipment each possesses for inseminating females. To put it delicately, daddy daddy long-legs have them and father spiders do not.

Salamanders: Dark Nights, March Rains

hen the first rains of spring shower upon the forest, spotted salamanders make ready to move. The leaves of autumn are soggy now, and upon them a few clumps of snow, stubbornly refusing to melt, lie scattered on the north-facing slopes of hills. As the cool rainwater turns the soil to mud, hordes of *Ambystoma maculatum*, the spotted salamander, set out for their ancestral breeding pools. Spotted salamanders often move in substantial numbers, although there is probably little if any coordination among individuals. But forward they go. Neither marching nor slithering nor crawling, spotted salamanders plod through the woods on short, chubby legs, dragging long fleshy tails behind them. The style of locomotion, impossible to describe in a single word, falls somewhere between a waddle and a drag.

Spotted salamanders usually appear in late March or early April. As wood frogs freshly emerged from their own hibernacula serenade mates in raucous chorus, the salamanders rise out of the spongy, freshly thawed earth. They have lived an underground life since the last mating season the previous spring. If the time of year is right but conditions are cold and dry, the salamanders will wait below the surface. The leaf litter in the forest is a good insulator. It helps keep the salamanders warm (at least as warm as an animal with antifreeze in its veins needs to be) and protects them from drying March winds. Sooner or later, however, the year's first warm shower begins to fall. A steady, gentle patter drums on the fallen leaves. That night, humans who brave the damp and chill and venture into the woods can witness one of the most remarkable mass movements in all of nature.

The male salamanders generally move first, sometimes several nights before the females. Summoned by the rain, the males rise from the leaf mold, orient themselves in the direction of the shallow fishless ponds where they will breed, and wriggle into motion. The trip to the pond from the point of emergence may take several hours, or perhaps longer. Along the way, the salamanders may encounter obstacles. The most troubling are those put in their way by humans—roads (in some places, hundreds of salamanders are squished by automobile tires on a single night), walls, and houses. The salamanders have been living on and under the hillsides we view as lawns and neighborhoods for countless millennia. They visit breeding pools used by their parents, grandparents, and far distant forebears.

Creatures of habit, salamanders do not readily change their ways. They are simple animals, but one must admire their determination. A spotted salamander bent on reaching its breeding pond is a diminutive, slowed-down version of a charging rhinoceros. It is not easily deterred.

Scattered throughout the woods where spotted salamanders live are small, shallow depressions. In summer, the mud in the bottoms of these may be as dry as baking flour, but in late winter when the snow melts and spring rains begin to fall, the depressions fill. Because they are short-lived, these vernal ponds rarely support populations of fish, turtles, and other potential predators of salamanders. Into such basins the spotted salamanders descend.

There is no getting around the fact that a spotted salamander is a comical-looking creature. About six inches in length from snout to tail, it is covered with smooth, jet-black skin. The skin is creased at regular intervals along the salamander's flanks, and from one end to the other it is marked with big yellow spots. A spotted salamander looks more like a beast of fancy— a creature in a storybook—than a genuine living animal.

Upon reaching the vernal ponds, the male salamanders slip quietly into the water. Their silence contrasts with the clamor of the wood frogs and the spring peepers that use the same pools for breeding. The sounds of the singing amphibians, distant cousins of the salamanders, are nearly deafening to human ears.

Spotted salamanders are excellent swimmers and can remain submerged for long periods. Once in the water, they stake out patches of pond bottom where they deposit their sperm in pea-size gelatinous packages called *spermatophores*. Spotted salamanders practice internal fertilization of an unusual sort. Rather than copulating directly with females, the male salamanders glue spermatophores to decaying leaves and submerged rocks, then await the arrival of the females. When the females come, the males try to persuade them to pick up their sperm as a cargo plane might take on some boxes.

Hours or several nights pass. Sometimes, in a dry spring when the March rains arrive later than usual, the migratory and nuptial activity of the spotted salamanders may be compressed into a single night. Sooner or later, at any rate, the females arrive, and the males are waiting to greet them. They meet in the water. A male selects a female and swims closely beside her. Other males may join the pursuit, and the most persistent is likely the successful suitor. In the water, the salamanders move gracefully, swimming in synchrony as if performing some sort of aquatic ballet.

When she is ready, the female glides to the bottom of the pool and picks up one or more of the male's spermatophores. She does this with the lips of her vent, or cloaca, an opening at the base of her tail that serves double duty in breeding and excretion. If all goes well, the sperm will fertilize her eggs, and sometime later she will exude them in a gelatinous mass. The mass is attached to the stem of a submerged branch. It is globular in shape, sometimes transparent, sometimes translucent. A flashlight beam trained on an egg mass illuminates the embryonic salamanders adrift in a sea of jelly.

Desires fulfilled, the male and female salamanders go their separate ways. The next rainy night they leave the pond, trusting their eggs to hatch in the cool water. The tadpolelike larvae develop without care or assistance. Back up the slopes the adult salamanders labor, crossing roads, circumventing boulders, and detouring around houses. Somewhere, somehow, they choose places to dig into the soil. From now on, the salamanders live like moles, feeding on grubs and worms and other creatures of the soil, until the cold weather of autumn halts their movements. Then they sleep. Day by day another winter will pass, the March rains will fall, and again it will be time for romance.

9

American Toads and their Courtship: Love and Warts

This is not, as the title suggests, another grim tale about a socially transmitted ailment. It is a story about toads.

Toads, like frogs, are members of the great amphibian order Anura. Toads begin life as eggs deposited in water. Before a mother toad lays her eggs, she must endure acrobatic advances by male toads. And the males are boorish lovers. They push and shove themselves upon females (and each other) with great gusto and not a shred of delicacy.

Observing a group of toads in a breeding pool is like watching a rumble between opposing high school football teams the Friday night before a game. It is difficult to separate the individual combatants. Piles of six, eight, or ten toads are not unusual. Somewhere buried in the heap one can usually find a female. She is generally larger than the offensive tacklers, perhaps because size is an advantage in fending off suitors. When the mood is right—generally when a single male has settled comfortably on her back—the female toad squeezes out a transparent gelatinous ribbon containing thousands of tiny eggs. The male fertilizes these as they emerge.

The eggs hatch and out come larvae. The larvae are big-headed, long-tailed, and legless. They look more like fish than the four-legged adults they will become. Most of us call the larvae "tadpoles" or "pollywogs."

The tadpoles of toads and frogs are very active. They feed voraciously. Many species in this stage dine entirely on plants, although some are carnivorous. Spadefoot toad tadpoles often eat each other. Eventually, the tadpoles mature, lose their tails, sprout legs, and emerge. For toads, this amazing metamorphosis takes place within a single season, sometimes in a matter of days. This short-lived adolescence is probably an adaptation to life on land, where small woodland breeding pools dry up in the summer sun. Bullfrogs, which live in big lakes and other permanent bodies of water, have no such worries. Bullfrog tadpoles grow to great size. They swim around the home pond for two or three years before adulthood strikes.

In the world and around the country, there are many different species of toads and frogs. Most people are familiar with the three most widely known groups: the so-called true toads, the so-called true frogs, and the treefrogs.

Treefrogs are easily separated from the rest. They are the only amphibians in America with suction cups on their feet. Two species are found in my home woods in the Northeast: the thumbnail-size spring peeper and the somewhat larger gray treefrog. Gray treefrogs are sometimes called tree toads. Their skin is rough and mottled, vaguely reminiscent of that of a toad. A close look at the suction cups on the ends of their long toes, however, reveals their true identity. No true toad is built for climbing.

The group called the true frogs includes the most familiar of our frogs. Included are the bullfrog (a voracious predator known to eat birds and mice), the green frog, the wood frog, and the handsomely spotted pickerel frog. All these frogs have wet and fairly smooth skin, and all have long, muscular rear legs that make them excellent jumpers.

True toads, for the most part, are large (several inches long) and plump. Their skin is fairly dry with a surface marked by conspicuous wartlike prominences. Unlike true frogs, toads have short, slender hind legs. They cannot make great bounds like their smooth-skinned cousins and thus are never invited to frog-jumping contests. A toad literally couldn't jump to save its life. And for the most part it doesn't need to.

Toads, you may be surprised to learn, are poisonous. No need to fear that the toad you find in the garden will sink its fangs into your ankles. The fangs don't exist. The skin of toads simply contains a mild poison that is distasteful to those animals that might consider toads as food—foxes, dogs, and weasels. Predators, when young, learn to leave toads alone. For example, a fox pup that bites into a toad will not be eager to repeat the ordeal.

In the nineteenth century, mountebanks who peddled quack cures at medicine shows would often be accompanied by young accomplices. At the proper moment, an accomplice would emerge from the crowd, take to the stage, and pretend to eat a toad before the gullible audience. Symptoms of distress would appear at once, and seizing this as an opportunity to demonstrate the miraculous powers of his elixir, the mountebank would flourish a bottle, administer his panacea to the sufferer, and swiftly effect a cure. This hallowed practice gives the English language the expression *toadeater*, or *toady*, defined as a false flatterer, a truckler to the rich or powerful.

I often pick up a toad myself, not to cure what ails me but to examine its warts. (Toad warts, by the way, are warts in name only. They are not contagious.) The reason for my doing so is not a matter of aesthetics, for even a toad fancier such as myself cannot deny that toads are ugly, but a question of identification. Two species of toad reside in my neck of the woods: the American and the Fowler's. They look alike, but the size and arrangement of their warts can be used to separate them.

So I look at the toad's back. If it is marked by blotches of dark skin, and a single large wart rises from each blotch, I am reasonably certain that the beast in hand is an American toad. If, however, each dark patch contains four or five smallish warts, the toad is probably a Fowler's. To confirm this assessment, I examine the hind legs. The thighs of American toads are brownish and prominently studded with large warts.

Fowler's toads have relatively smooth thighs crossed by dark bands.

Before I place the toad back on the ground it will probably urinate in my palm. I'm used to this and never horrified. After all, if I were picked up by a giant a hundred times my size, I would probably do the same.

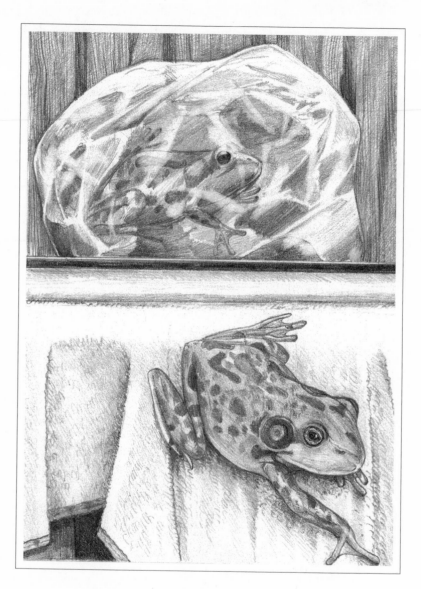

10

A Frog with Antifreeze: Out of the Icebox and into the Frying Pan

irst days of work at new jobs are often memorable. Eleven years ago, for example, on my first day on the staff of a particular nature center, I was assigned a desk in an "office" that housed an assortment of venomous and nonvenomous snakes. My desk was pushed into a corner, nestled beside the cages of harmless species. In the desk, in a deep drawer that smelled of something musty, I found a large frog. The frog was dead. Its skin had turned a ghastly black, and its legs were extended as if it had died in mid-leap. Apparently the poor fellow had been dead so long that he was entirely desiccated, for he gave off no odor of decay.

Naturally, I asked my colleagues about the frog. Ah, we'd wondered where he'd got to, they said, discussing the corpse as if he were an old and treasured friend. There's a story behind that frog. Would you like to hear it? A pot of coffee was brewed, and the story was told. It went something like this.

One winter day, on the rigid crystalline surface of a nearby lake, a naturalist was teaching a group of children about life in a frozen pond. Snow was cleared from a place to get a look at the ice below, and voilà! There were two frogs, imbedded in the ice like flies stuck in amber. The children took a great interest in the amphibians, so the naturalist grabbed an ice chisel and, leaving a wide margin of safety so as not to disturb the frogs themselves, chipped out a block of ice that held the animals in the center.

Everyone (including the naturalist) wanted to know if the frogs could possibly be alive. There was only one way to find out. The block of ice was carried back to the nature center and placed on a chair near a woodstove to melt very slowly.

One of the frogs was dead. When the last glistening wedges of ice fell away from its body it was limp and rubbery.

But shortly after the last of the ice had turned to water, the other frog began to twitch. In a few minutes it was sitting on its haunches (as frogs like to do), blinking its eyes, and looking hardly the worse for its ordeal.

The scientific explanation behind the frog's resurrection is fairly straightforward. In northerly climes, the blood of amphibians contains an antifreeze that is little different in its chemical composition from the Prestone that motorists use to protect the cooling systems of their automobiles. Because their blood incorporates this antifreeze, frogs, toads, and salamanders can survive subfreezing temperatures, at least up to a point. The dead frog had passed that point, apparently, but its luckier comrade had not and thus managed to teach thirty boys and girls a dramatic lesson in survival.

After the class returned to its school, the frog that had risen from the dead became a celebrity. He was housed in his own private aquarium, placed on public view, and fattened on a rich diet of crickets, mealworms, and ground beef. Unfortunately, the story does not end here. One night, while his human protectors were at home asleep in their beds, the frog escaped from his quarters. His absence was noticed first thing the next morning and a search party was organized. Closets were opened, bookshelves were emptied, and dusty corners were explored. No sign of the frog could be found.

A telltale odor might have been detected in the nature center in the weeks that followed, but it was not. Nature centers are places of myriad smells—the musk of snakes, the must of old books, the woodsy aroma of naturalists who earn their livings in swamps and forests—and a single odor (even if it is a new one, and even if it is unpleasant) is not easily distinguished. No one found the frog for months.

Then, one day in early spring, someone happened to peer behind a radiator and spy a dark motionless form. It proved to be the resurrected frog. This time there was no reviving him, for the poor fellow had been completely dehydrated by heat from the radiator. The naturalists and office workers at the nature center had grown fond of the frog, and no one had the heart to dispose of him. So the mummy was put in the drawer in which I discovered him, and there, I imagine, he remains.

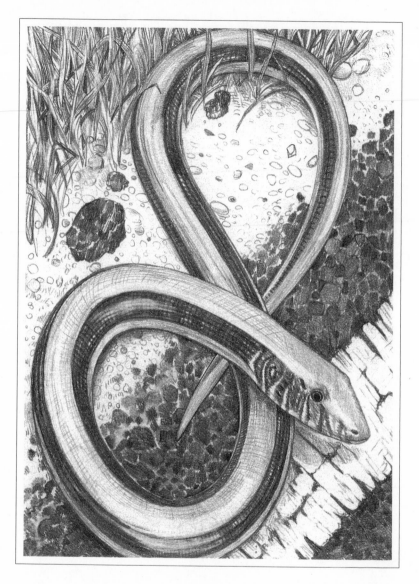

11

The Evolution of Snakes, or A Farewell to Arms

Snakes evolved from their four-legged forebears into the slithering cylindrical creatures we know today as snakes sometime during the Jurassic period—150 million years ago, or thereabouts. For reptiles, these were good old days. Plesiosaurs and ichthyosaurs cavorted in warm oceans, dinosaurs and pterosaurs were still fresh faces on the world scene, and sphenodontids (relatives of New Zealand's tuatara, a lizardlike beast that is a sort of terrestrial coelacanth) inhabited most of the planet's dry land. Lizards were already abundant and wide ranging. They had evolved much earlier than the snakes and were well on their way toward diverging into familiar sidelines such as the iguanas and the geckos. The age of reptiles was in full swing, and snakes were about to join the party.

Sometime late in the Jurassic, one group of early lizards left the main street of evolution and turned into a developmental road not taken. This group, according to paleontologists and taxonomists, gave rise to the snakes. (Taxonomists do not work for the Internal Revenue Service. They are scientists who divide living things into groups, or *taxa*.)

Taxonomists sometimes squabble over which roadmap the ancestors of snakes followed to become snakes, but they stand together regarding which of the scaled reptiles, or squamates, can be labeled snakes. The criteria they use (and do not use) in distinguishing between snakes and lizards may surprise you. Even an expert, for example, cannot tell a snake from a lizard by the presence or absence of legs. No snake has front legs or arms, but several, such as the boas and pythons, have rear legs. This astonishing fact can be confirmed by visiting your neighborhood snake fancier. (Every town has one.) Examine the man's thirteen-foot Burmese python or the boa constrictor that hangs around his neck. Find the snake's excretory pore, or cloaca. And there, projecting from each side of the opening, you will find tiny vestigial legs, each tipped with a claw. For this reason, a scientific treatise on the evolution of snakes might be titled "A Farewell to Arms" but not "A Farewell to Arms and Legs."

To be fair, boas and pythons should not shoulder—or in any way bear—the entire burden of guilt for blurring the distinctions between lizards and snakes. Just as there are snakes such as boas and pythons that possess legs, there are lizards that lack them. The glass lizards of the southern United States, for example, are entirely limbless. They look like short, robust snakes or overfed worms. But they are genuine lizards, for reasons we will address in a moment. Glass lizards are so-named because their tails can shatter into fragments when the animals are dropped or mishandled.

Anyone who has watched the film *Raiders of the Lost Ark* has seen legless lizards in abundance. As the story reaches its crescendo, the hero, Indiana Jones, finds himself at the bottom of a pit. There he is met by several large, inquisitive cobras and thousands of small slithering "snakes." According to a herpetologist friend of mine, the smaller serpents were bogus—not snakes at all but harmless glass lizards that were employed to masquerade as the real thing.

Hold a glass lizard in your hand, watch closely, and you may see it blink. You may also notice small, dark openings in the skin behind each of the glass lizard's eyes. These openings are external ears. Now you know you're looking at a lizard for sure. No snake can blink, for none has movable eyelids, and no snake has external ears.

Yet even the presence or absence of eyelids and ear holes does not offer a foolproof basis on which to separate snakes and lizards. Some burrowing lizards have fixed eyelids. A few lizards have no external ears. Clearly, differentiating snakes and lizards is not an easy business, and the taxonomists who do so merit our sympathy. In the end, they are forced to rely on skeletal features too arcane to address here. Suffice it to say that a good taxonomist knows a snake when he sees one. He looks at the reptile's skull, and particularly at its backbone. Each snake vertebra possesses features called *accessory articulating surfaces* that lizard vertebrae lack. These are known, rather poetically, as the *zygosphene* and the *zygantrum*. The earliest known snake, described from a skull and backbone that are well preserved as fossils, is *Dinilysia*. This reptile is known from 80-million-year-old rocks deposited in South America during the Upper Cretaceous period.

Snakes such as *Dinilysia*, it's agreed, evolved from lizards. But why? And how? Here taxonomists and evolutionary theorists find spirited disagreement. The standard explanation—one I've delivered myself to hundreds of credulous schoolchildren—is that snakes passed through a burrowing stage during their evolution. According to this point of view, movable eyelids, limbs for walking, and outer ears were of little advantage to lizards that lived underground. In fact, such features were downright hindrances. Thus, selective pressure, working over millions of years, resulted in the elimination of eyelids, limbs, and outer ears and led to their replacement by other more useful features—gogglelike eye coverings, flexible backbones, and specialized muscles useful for crawling and climbing. According to theory, these features lingered (and continue to linger) long after most snakes returned to lives on the surface.

This, at any rate, is the *old* theory. Today, evolutionary theorists are not so sure snakes evolved under cover. A recent book on the evolution of vertebrates by the Canadian paleontologist Robert L. Carroll suggests problems with this view. The skulls of burrowing lizards, according to Carroll, contain rigid assemblages of bones, making them quite unlike the flexible, elastic skulls of snakes. One might have expected members of the lizard underground to possess skulls similar to those of snakes, but this is not the case. Another troublesome point: the earliest fossil snakes, and the first fossil "intermediates" between lizards and snakes, seem not to have been burrowing animals at all. Apparently, they lived in water and their skulls were highly flexible.

Dr. Carroll adds a modicum of clarity to the muddle with a few well-considered ideas. The loss of outer ears by snakes may not have resulted from taking up an underground life but have arisen as a by-product during the evolution of a mobile jaw. Such a jaw allows a snake to swallow animals whole, even some that are larger than its own head. (I once saw a man in a McDonald's restaurant try to perform a similar feat.) This skill is useful in a world where the intervals between meals may be long. A snake with a big, flexible mouth can devour a week's sustenance in a single greedy bite.

Similarly, the loss of eyelids by snakes may not have required a subterranean phase. Some mammals underwent similar changes in their visual paraphernalia—not because they took up underground lives but as a spinoff of evolving night vision. Snakes, Dr. Carroll suggests, evolved as nocturnal creatures. Their brand of eye—a simple reduced structure with a clear protective covering and no movable lid—was well adapted to a life spent wriggling over the ground, scraping past rocks, plant stems, and abrasive soil.

Conflicting theories aside, snakes evolved, one way or another, and they dispersed and diversified with great success. Today, around the world, there are some 2,389 species, including over 1,400 species in the Colubridae—the family that includes most of North America's nonvenomous snakes—alone. A few snakes grow large enough to eat goats and pigs. Others are tiny and delicate, growing no longer or thicker around than a pencil. And many, such as the pit vipers and the cobras, are poisonous. All snakes, of course, have as much right to slither over the earth as we do, and they are worthy of our respect, our interest, and—as fellow travelers in the journey of life—our affection.

12

Rattlesnakes and Cottonmouths: A Secret in the Pits

This is a story about pits. Not the kind of pits found inside apples, nor the sort inflicted upon skin by acne, nor the bottomless variety, nor the kind unpleasant to inhabit (as in "This place is the pits!"), nor the late movie actress named Zasu whose surname, Pitts, carried an extra consonant. This is a story about the pits that occur in the faces of certain snakes—the pit vipers, the boas, and the pythons.

To survive in this dog-eat-dog and snake-eat-mouse world, animals have evolved an array of senses with which to keep an eye, or an ear, or a nose on each other. Some animals smell. Others see. A great many hear. The really sensuous ones taste and touch. But there is a sixth sense, a sense possessed by rattlesnakes and their kin, and by boas and pythons: the ability to detect differences in temperature, to see wavelengths in the infrared end of the spectrum. The organs that are involved in perceiving this sixth sense are housed in pits. Boas and pythons have pits in single rows just above the edge of their upper lips, one set on each side of the head. Pit vipers (rattlesnakes, copperheads, cottonmouths, and their Latin American relations) have a single pit beside each nostril.

Pits are useful to serpents that hunt chiefly at night. Up to a point, snakes track prey animals by their distinctive scents. Beyond that point—the point where a prospective meal is "close at hand" (for lack of an apt expression)—the snake needs a more sophisticated, finely tuned sense to guide its final lunge. Here the ability to sense infrared light (heat) proves its mettle.

The system works like this. A copperhead slithers toward a mouse or, more likely, a mouse ventures unwittingly close to a copperhead. When the two are a foot or so apart, the snake discerns that the temperature of the mouse is warmer than that of the environment. The process works much the same if the prospective meal is a cold-blooded animal, such as a frog. Amphibians have moist skin from which water is continually evaporating. As the water vaporizes, heat is absorbed and the amphibian's skin is cooled. Thus the surface temperature of a frog is lower than the temperature of its environment, and the copperhead with pits in its face can sense the difference.

The copperhead has two pits, and the range of sensation of each overlaps that of the other. This means that the snake scans the world of warmth and coolness stereoscopically. Much as human eyes see in three dimensions, thus judging distance as well as horizontal and vertical positioning, a copperhead detects differences in temperature in three dimensions. Because of this talent, a copperhead in total darkness can make a blind strike that is perfectly on target.

The infrared sense of snakes is incredibly, well, *sensitive*. Snake pits (the facial kind) are lined with infrared-triggered cells in great number; as many as fifteen hundred may cover each square millimeter of a pit's delicate lining. Working as a team, these cells detect differences in temperature between meal and milieu as minuscule as two one-thousandths of a degree Fahrenheit.

As a human, I admire snakes for their pits, and for their marvelous sixth sense. Admittedly, however, if I were a mouse or a frog, I might see the pits in a different light.

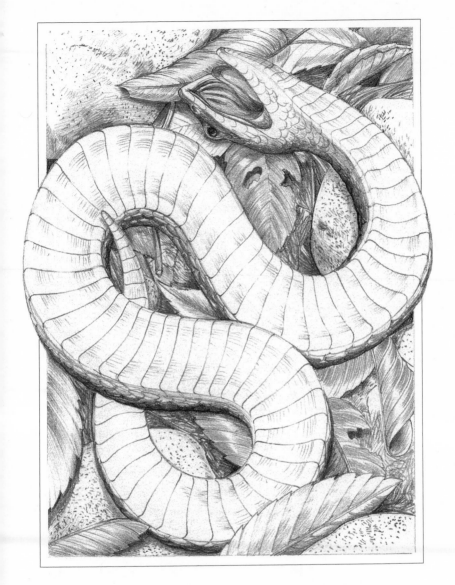

13

Hognose Snakes: Pure Bluff

Among small- to medium-size reptiles, not one—neither a rattlesnake, nor a cobra, nor a Gila monster—puts on a more convincing display of ferocity than a hognose snake. Stumble upon one of these cowardly lions in a field or forest, and it will do its serpentine best to frighten you in toto. Unless you've caught the act before, you'll probably run or scream; and no matter how experienced you are, you may think twice about stepping closer. As the snake advances, mouth gaping, hissing viciously, its broad head and upper body sculpted into a sinister, cobralike hood, this Bert Lahr of the reptile world cuts a rather formidable figure. It rears off the ground, apparently poised to strike.

As Dorothy did in Oz, you may call the bully's bluff. Step forward and grab a hognose snake by the midriff (close your eyes, if you must). Assuming you've identified the animal correctly (hope that you have), instead of fangs sinking into your arm, you'll soon feel a taut, scaly body turning limp within your grasp. This ends Act One. Hognose snakes, when confronted, are quickly deflated. They are, truth be told, no more lionhearted than a man in a lion suit.

Nor, apparently, do hognose snakes possess much in the way of brains. Take a hognose that has gone soft in your hands (it's playing dead) and place it on its belly on the ground. What then? Remove your fingers. The snake will roll over on its back. You may think that the snake has expired of fright and the roll was just a dying reflex. The mouth hangs open, the forked tongue hangs limp, and blood oozes from the snake's palate. A witch with a farmhouse on her head could not look more sincerely dead. But just to be sure, turn the snake over.

Again it will roll on its back. A second dying reflex, you wonder? Turn it again. And again the snake rolls. Ah, you now see, there is madness in its method. This actor has gotten the idea that dead snakes never lie on their bellies. So convinced is the hognose of this, in fact, that nothing you can do will persuade it otherwise.

Now for the truth about hognose snakes, now that you have been daring enough to handle one: they're venomous. Sort of. Eastern hognose snakes dine almost exclusively upon toads. Occasionally, when necessity presses, one will condescend to take a frog or salamander, but toads are the hognose snake's daily bread. When a snake latches on to a warty meal, the main course is less than pleased. The toad fights back but is eventually persuaded to accept its fate by an injection of mild venom. The teeth that do the injecting are located in the back of the snake's mouth. In this position, the fangs are of use in subduing toads but have no value in inflicting misery upon animals as large and fast-moving as humans.

So have no fear. When face-to-face with a hognose snake, you must remember this: a hiss is just a hiss.

14
The Northern Copperhead

T he quiet suburban neighborhood where I grew up consists of several dozen Cape Cod houses surrounded by green lawns that manifest various stages of takeover by crabgrass and dandelions. The yards of the homes fit together like pieces in a jigsaw puzzle, and in their haphazard agglomeration they fully cover the west flank of a ridge. Over the hill, the eastern slope of the ridge is raw and wild (preserved as a watershed), so that the street on which I grew up, which runs along the ridge's spine, has something of the feel of a frontier. In addition to the usual squirrels, chipmunks, toads, and songbirds that inhabit suburban communities, our neighborhood was blessed with an abundance of poisonous snakes—fat, slow-moving northern copperheads that had a talent for getting themselves killed by automobiles.

Growing up, I learned quickly that the name "copperhead" struck fear into the hearts of my chipmunk-loving, serpento-phobic neighbors. No one knew, or cared to know, that the copperheads were calm, retiring creatures that rarely struck with their fangs even when disturbed, or that copperhead venom is mild compared to that of rattlers, cobras, and coral snakes. Nor did anyone take the time to notice that copperheads, with their handsome geometric markings and burnished colors, are stunningly beautiful. The snakes were poisonous, that was the main thing. Among my neighbors, killing one was considered heroic and philanthropic, like the slaying of a dragon.

During the 1930s, Raymond Ditmars, a long-time curator of reptiles for the New York Zoological Society, made several collecting trips to our rocky ridge. On one such occasion, he captured a copperhead that measured fifty-three inches in length. While the black rat snakes that climb our trees grow perhaps twice as long, fifty-three inches is huge for a copper-head. In fact, the snake caught by Ditmars may well be the largest specimen of *Agkistrodon contortrix* ever recorded.

Copperheads still abounded in the area during the years when I was growing up. This can be said with certainty because as kids we found many of them flattened on neighborhood streets. Sometimes the snakes were freshly dead, still oozing blood. More often, however, by the time it was found, a cop-perhead was baked by the sun to the color and consistency of old leather. The great number of corpses meant that the snakes were numerous, but in seventeen years I never saw a copper-head alive.

This is not to say that we didn't search for them. My friends and I were savvy enough to know that copperheads sunned themselves in spring and fall on rock outcrops. We searched such places in the watershed woods year after year. To my knowledge, not one of us ever set eyes on a real live specimen, either by design or by accident. And certainly no one was ever bitten or chased up a tree.

We *did* succeed in catching an occasional water snake. The result was always the same: my friends would insist that the hapless serpent was a copperhead, if for no other reason than subduing a fearsome copperhead was far more exciting than capturing anything else. According to a script that was acted out again and again, I would protest that the captive was merely a harmless water snake, displaying what I considered to be great erudition in identifying reptiles. In the end the mob's opinion would win the day. The snake was declared a copper-head, and a death sentence was pronounced.

Over the years I watched in horror and disgust as at least a dozen water snakes were senselessly executed. There are no limits to the gruesome means boys can invent for snuffing out the life of an ostensible adversary. Snakes were drowned, or chopped in pieces (for maximum effect, beginning at the tail and working forward), or placed in a jar that was connected to the exhaust pipe of a lawn mower. In each case the result was the death of the snake.

One wonders where children learn such barbaric behavior. In this case, at least, my friends were simply mimicking adults. Several grownups in our neighborhood, reasonable people by other standards, made a regular habit of chopping up snakes with hoes, spades, and shovels. Mercy was something a snake—especially a poisonous snake, and every snake was assumed to be poisonous even if a know-it-all kid claimed otherwise—did not deserve.

Eager herpetologist that I was, I investigated snake mutilations whenever word reached me of their occurrence. Often I was too late to find out much because the garbageman had hurried off with the evidence. Yet sometimes I succeeded in getting a look at the victim, and never once in all those years was the dead snake actually a copperhead. Again and again, black rat snakes, garters, and milk snakes suffered the ultimate penalty for mistaken identity: death by guillotine.

One might get the idea that people in our neighborhood didn't know what copperheads looked like. Not true. They did. Copperheads were squashed on the road each summer. Everyone had seen them. But when confronted with live snakes, common sense vanished, and all snakes became copperheads.

The snakes that were killed were always said to possess the classic copperhead features: a head shaped like an arrowhead, a plump coppery-colored body, and hourglass markings. Yet the victim, when I got a look at it, was sure to be black, striped, or marked with rectangular, brick-colored blotches and a checkerboard belly. "Look, sonny," I was told on one occasion by a neighbor who had just bludgeoned a nonvenomous reptile. *"That* is a copperhead!" No amount of explanation on my part ever succeeded in convincing the crusading serpent slayer otherwise.

One day when I was ten or eleven, I came upon a man along the shore of a nearby reservoir who was in the process of killing a water snake with a stick. He explained to me that the snake was a water moccasin. I explained to him that water moccasins were southern snakes, and that to find one he would have to drive all the way to Virginia. He told me to get lost.

At some point during my early years, a neighbor managed to convince me that copperheads smelled like rotten cucumbers. It wasn't long before I began to detect rotten cucumber odor just about everywhere—despite the fact that I had no idea how a rotten cucumber smelled. Although I was a defender of copperheads, I was still a bit afraid of them. In one place in our backyard at the base of a stone wall, the fearsome "cucumber" odor seemed particularly strong. Day after day, year after year, I checked the spot. I never found a snake. Apparently, whatever was the source of the smell, it wasn't a copperhead.

For all the fear and loathing, no one on the street was ever bitten by a copperhead. Surely the copperheads had plenty of opportunity. As kids we climbed rock faces supposedly infested with snakes, tromped through brushy woods by day and by night, and fished baseballs and Frisbees out of dark places where we probably shouldn't have stuck our hands. In all those years, there wasn't a single case of snakebite.

The only copperhead incident of note involved a dog, an aged and arthritic Chihuahua named Tiny. Tiny achieved instant celebrity one bright spring morning by stepping out a door and landing squarely upon the real McCoy. The copperhead, coiled and perhaps asleep, was soaking up heat from a sun-warmed flagstone. No longer keen of sight, Tiny blundered upon the snake and was bitten. The dog's owners quickly realized what had happened. They killed the snake so they could show its corpse to the veterinarian. Tiny herself staggered back into the house and collapsed on the floor.

At the vet's office, Tiny, who was already beginning to revive, was given a shot of Dramamine. I was called in to identify the snake. Yes, it really was a copperhead. I dissected the snake's stomach. Inside was a gypsy moth caterpillar. Tiny went back and lived out the rest of her days with no further trouble from snakes. But the word got around—I made sure of that. The terrible scourge of our neighborhood, the fearsome copperhead, had failed to harm a Chihuahua.

15
A Rattlesnake
in the Grass

The snake, all five feet of it, lies coiled beside a hummock. Overhead, the long narrow leaves of sedges define arcs against an ultramarine sky. The ends of the sedge leaves hang over the snake, concealing it in the same incomplete but effective way that bangs hide a forehead.

Thirty feet away, across a narrow brook that trickles past the hummock, a young man and a young woman, both wielding binoculars, admire a bird. The bird is colored yellow with a black hood and bib, and the two observers recognize it as a hooded warbler. The man, among other things, is a writer. The woman, among other things, is a friend of the man.

A forked tongue darts out twice and is twice retracted.

The snake has a sculpted head, thicker than the portion of the torso from which it bulges. The head is covered with scales, each meticulously defined. The scales are colored a sickly yellow-olive, something like the color of gangrene.

The bird vanishes. The man and woman turn, aiming toward the trail from which they wandered. A gust of cool air passes low over the meadow, rustling the sedges. Spring has arrived, and the wind is heavy with fragrance and pollen.

A forked tongue darts out twice and is twice retracted.

The snake, because it has no eyelids, stares. It gazes stoically at the man and the woman, who are approaching. The ground throbs with the pounding of human feet, and the snake feels the vibrations. For some reason fathomable only to itself, the snake does not shake its tail. The man, who walks ahead of the woman, is now within a foot of the snake.

A forked tongue darts out twice and is twice retracted.

The snake's tail culminates in a series of translucent knobs. These, if shaken, would produce a loud rattling. But the snake remains motionless, making no sounds. The man's left leg and foot come toward the snake. They pass within three inches of the scaly head, brushing the leaves of the sedges. They come to rest on the hummock, compressing it like a spring. The snake can sense the man's warmth. The man is oblivious to the presence of the snake.

A forked tongue darts out twice and is twice retracted.

The snake lies utterly still, more like a sculpture of a snake than a living thing. Its neck forms a double curve, like the letter S. The snake is very much alive, however. Its heart beats, and its single attenuated lung inflates and empties.

The man's right foot and leg come toward the snake. Passing within three inches of the snake's head, the foot brushes the leaves of the sedges. The leg reaches out beyond the hummock and comes to rest on a stone. Close behind the man, the woman follows.

A forked tongue darts out twice and is twice retracted.

The snake has not moved, but the woman, observant, discerns its shape beneath the sedges, and she hesitates. The man is now about as far beyond the hummock as she is from reaching it—eight feet. "Did you know that you just stepped over a big snake?" she says.

"What kind of snake?"

"I don't know. A big one."

Carefully, the man circles back, crossing the brook on a different set of hummocks. He expects to see a water snake, fat and mud-colored, or a black racer, long and broomstick-thin with a torso rising out of the grass in a perfect *sine* curve. Instead, peeking through the curtain of sedges, he sees *Crotalus horridus*. He has encountered dozens of timber rattlesnakes at close quarters, but this is the longest, the heaviest, the most formidable.

The man turns ashen. Inside his chest his heart starts to pound. At no time in his life has he ever felt more lucky, or more grateful. Quickly, the man and the woman leave the meadow. They have lost their taste for birdwatching there, and without argument they will concede the place to the rattlesnake.

A forked tongue darts out twice and is twice retracted.

PART FOUR

Odds and Ends
(Mostly Odds)

1
Checkerboard Flounder

Birds do it. Certain lizards and frogs do it. Even overeducated fish that spend their entire lives in schools do it. Change color, that is.

Birds change plumages nearly as often as fashion-conscious teenagers switch brands of sneakers. They shed one set of feathers and grow another, and there is no law of nature that says the second set must match the hues of the first. The male wood duck, for example, spends the greater part of the year in plumage so colorful, so magnificent in its intricate details, that even the most flamboyant parrot of the Amazon might envy him. In summer, however, the wood duck drake opts for camouflage drab. He sheds his colors, then spends the next several weeks looking as if he had been dunked in mud. At this time ornithologists say that the male wood duck is in "eclipse."

But eclipses are brief, and soon the wood duck is sprouting a shiny new duplicate of his original regalia. The exact reason why the male wood duck passes through the eclipse stage is unknown. If there is a Mother Nature, perhaps she is putting an annual limit on the swelling of the wood duck's ego.

Aside from annual changes in plumage, other birds begin their lives as one color, then switch hues when they grow up. Little blue herons, for example, are white as youngsters and resemble their cousin egrets more than they do their own parents. Only as adults do little blues acquire their eponymous plumes. There are other examples. Bald eagles aren't bald for their first few years, red-tailed hawk youngsters aren't immediately red in the tail, and juvenile starlings lack their parents' galaxy of spots.

In birds, color changes are not restricted to plumage. Young snowy egrets have black feet, but the feet turn yellow when the birds grow up. Adult sharp-shinned and Cooper's hawks have yellow eyes when immature, red eyes as adults. One of the most dramatic makeovers of all occurs in cattle egrets. Look at a flock of these camp followers distributed across a pasture, and you will see that some of the birds (the young ones) have yellow bills, yellow eyes, and black legs, while others (the breeding adults) have orange bills, red eyes, and pink legs.

Scientists consider the bird a higher order of beast than the reptile, the amphibian, and the fish, but in matters of color change the so-called lower orders put the higher orders to shame. A flounder, for example, changes the colors of its skin to match the pattern and hue of the ocean bottom upon which it lives. It does this not by magic but by altering the pigments in skin cells called chromatophores. So complete is the flounder's ability to mimic a background that if you put one in an aquarium with a checkerboard bottom, the flounder's skin would soon appear as a mosaic of black and white squares.

Among amphibians, dozens of species change color with aplomb, and often on the spur of the moment. Spring peepers and gray treefrogs, for example, can appear green one minute, brown the next, and gray a minute after that. Political candidates often accuse each other of changing their colors as if it were something to be ashamed of; it isn't. In the real world, changing color is a matter of survival, and survival is the first priority of all of us—peepers and politicians included. The most famous color switcher of all is the chameleon. The chameleon is an Old World lizard that can hang by its tail, move its eyeballs independently of each other, and take on a new color at the drop of a hat. In the United States, chameleons are found only as pets, but their distant relations, the anoles of our South, can alter their appearance just as dramatically.

A colleague of mine had a friend with a pet anole. The lizard lived on the man's curtains, using its sticky tongue to snatch flies and other insects that were attracted to the sunlight that the curtains partially kept out. Although a helpful pet, the anole wasn't much company. It blended so perfectly with the colors and weave of the curtains that his owner could rarely find him.

The moral: if you want to see your pet flounder, be careful where you put your checkerboard.

2
Among the Javelina, or How I Joined a Herd of Swine

When you're out of work, short on cash, and blue, as I often am these days, you feel a sudden attraction for the herd. Marching to a different drummer, once a source of great personal satisfaction, now only makes you sore. You long to fall into line with others, to join a herd. Any herd will do. The Moonies, the Goonies, the Churchgoers, the Dirt Throwers—all are as different as years in a century, but each offers the same opportunity to join, to share, to move in a group, to be carried along unthinkingly by the group's own collective momentum. There is nothing wrong with any of this. The herding instinct is as natural as the urge to eat, and at times it may be necessary for survival.

Recently, during a short holiday in the Chisos Mountains of West Texas, I availed myself of an opportunity to join a herd. I was exploring a dry, cactus-studded gully in Big Bend National Park when I heard grunting sounds coming from behind some bushes. Venturing closer, I began to hear the sounds from all sides. Before I realized the predicament in which I had placed myself, I was surrounded by fifteen or twenty wild piglike animals called javelina.

Javelina, for the unacquainted, are not pigs at all but belong to a small, select family of New World mammals called tayassuids. There are two species in the group: the white-lipped peccary, which ranges from Central America to Paraguay, and the collared peccary, or javelina, which ranges from southern Texas and southern Arizona all the way to Patagonia. Unlike genuine pigs, peccaries are small mammals. They have straight tusks, single dewclaws, and two-part stomachs, and they rarely weigh more than sixty pounds. On their backs, hidden in coarse fur, peccaries have glands that give off a musky odor much like the bouquet of skunks.

Several of the javelina grunted loudly, eyeing me suspiciously. I stood my ground. Before long the surprise of my appearance seemed to wear off, and I was able to roam among the animals freely. Together the javelina and I snuffled and shuffled our way up a hillside. My dark, self-absorbed companions paused now and again to urinate and to munch on cactus fruits while I, feeling particularly privileged, simply basked in their ready acceptance of my company. Occasionally my nostrils filled with javelina body odor, and I found the smell strong but not unpleasant. Scientists think that the odor of javelina may help bind the herds together. Keeping this in mind, I inhaled the essence gladly. At the time, I was feeling rejected by human society, and I was grateful that these beasts had granted me honorary entry to their band.

Over the ensuing hour, my cloven-hooved friends and I picked our way back downslope to a shady place beneath the overhanging limbs of a tree. Here, in a manner that impressed me with its civility, the javelina took turns sprawling one at a time in a wallow they had dug. The hole was filled with mud, despite the dryness of the surrounding country, and in it the pigs rolled. I listened closely, noting that while each javelina enjoyed the wallow, it made sounds of contentment that reminded me of the chugging of a steam engine.

I had reached a turning point. It was time for me either to take my turn in the wallow, thus initiating myself as a member of the troupe, or to rejoin my fellow *Homo sapiens* in the campground. Of course, there was never really any question of what I would do. My wife was waiting for me and we had plans for the day. Nevertheless, leaving was difficult. I inhaled deeply, gave the mudhole and my swinish comrades a last hard look, turned my back, and climbed alone out of the gully.

Barnum Was Wrong about Suckers

ike the comedian Rodney Dangerfield, the freshwater
fish known as the sucker gets no respect. When a
trout fisherman catches a sucker, he throws it back.
Bass fishermen do the same, and even kids have no
use for suckers. Fortunately for both the fish and the
fisherman, the accidental capture of a sucker is a rare event.
Suckers are bottom feeders for whom dry flies and bass plugs
hold little interest.

With its peculiar downward-facing mouth, fleshy lips,
slimy skin, and broad coarse scales, the sucker inspires universal revulsion. How strange, then, to read Henry David
Thoreau's thoughts about the fish. To the observant and
thoughtful Concord naturalist, the lowly sucker was a living
manifestation not of the gruesome but of the sublime.

Thoreau was the sucker's champion, although he once
wrote that cooked suckers tasted "like boiled brown paper." In
his journal he observed:

> The sight of the sucker floating on the meadow at this season [spring]
> affects me singularly, as if it were a fabulous or mythological fish,
> realizing my idea of a fish. It reminds me of pictures of dolphins or
> of Proteus. I see it for what it is,—not an actual terrene fish, but the
> fair symbol of a divine idea, the design of an artist.

Anyone who has at one time or another set eyes on a sucker
will know that Thoreau was laying it on a bit thick. Yet greater
praise was still to come. In the same journal entry, the world's
most famous pencil maker turned naturalist and ichthyologist
expanded upon his earlier theme:

> Its [the sucker's] color and form, its gills and fins and scales, are per-
> fectly beautiful, because they completely express to my mind what
> they were intended to express. . . . Such a form as is sculptured on
> ancient monuments and will be to the end of time. . . .

Thoreau has a point, although until one afternoon last spring, I would not have conceded it.

Before that fateful day, I shared the majority view that suckers are revolting. If I went fishing, the last thing I wanted on the end of my line was a sucker. The only time I ever hooked a sucker I brought it home to eat—not with steamed vegetables, but with misgivings. The way the sucker allowed itself to be hauled in like a wet shoe had seemed cowardly and undignified. On the bank, the fish was not pretty to look at. But I was curious to know how a sucker would taste, so the fish rode home in my tackle box.

I skinned and gutted the fish, which was about a foot long. It was dinnertime, but I couldn't bring myself to transfer the oily, flaccid carcass directly into the frying pan. So I put the sucker in the freezer. There it remained for a year, perhaps two. One day someone, probably my mother, discovered the fish and threw it in the trash. An opportunity had been lost; I never found out if Thoreau was right about suckers tasting like boiled paper.

My change of heart came one spring day many years later. I was walking beside a pond when chance provided me with an opportunity to watch suckers mating. I was stunned by what I saw. In fact, I swallowed so much humble pie that morning that I must now acknowledge suckers for what they really are: graceful creatures of enormous passion.

What did I see? The clear waters of the pond teemed with suckers. There were dozens of them, perhaps hundreds, moving to and fro in glittering swarms. Several feet from where I stood, a stream swollen by a heavy rain the night before poured over a gravel bar and emptied into the deep basin of the pond. Here, in the stream mouth, I saw the suckers mating. Three fish were swimming closely together, snouts into the current. I recognized them as suckers by their conspicuous stripes and trademark mouths. All were of similar size—about fifteen inches from snout to tail. As if the suckers were performers in a choreographed dance, they edged closer and closer to each other, adjusting their positions in the current. Each time a fish moved forward, a wave of energy moved down its body, beginning at the head, sweeping down its middle, and culminating in a brisk swish of the tail. After a dozen or so seconds, the flanks of the suckers touched. Their bodies were in perfect alignment.

What happened next nearly made my eyes pop out. The suckers began to thrash violently in the water while somehow keeping perfectly aligned with each other. As they shook, their white stripes turned fiery red and their eyes, also turning red, bulged as if ready to burst. The whole thing struck me as fantastic, and I might have thought I'd imagined it had not a 1920 Michigan study of suckers by Jacob Reighard turned up the same behavior. Like me, Reighard observed a *ménage à trois*. He noted that the sucker in the middle was a female and the ones on the outside were males. During the time when the three fish shook violently in synchrony, the males dispensed their milt, or sperm, and simultaneously, Reighard hypothesized, the female probably released her eggs.

I watched, unbelieving at first, as the suckers consummated their courtship, not merely once but again and again. Never had I seen a reproductive ritual in the animal world that could match such a spectacle. (The drumming of ruffed grouse and the tree bashing of rutting whitetail deer are tame in comparison.) And the scene *could* have been even wilder. Ichthyologists have witnessed female suckers mating with up to ten males, all at the same time. The Puritan in me shudders to think of this, but the libertine in me smiles.

Phineas "P. T." Barnum, who was not much of an ichthyologist, said "There's a sucker born every minute." The words are famous but woefully inaccurate. For one thing, suckers aren't born, at least in the traditional sense. They hatch. Matronly (but passionate) mother suckers have been known to produce as many as 40,000 eggs in a single unloading. After the expelled eggs are fertilized, those that are not accidentally damaged or eaten by predators hatch a few days later. In springtime, not one but hundreds of tiny suckers are "born" every minute.

Soon after emergence, the hatchling suckers (properly termed *fry*) begin nibbling on the scum that covers the surface of streams and ponds. Here they ingest microscopic plants and animals such as protozoa, diatoms, insects, and algae. Little suckers grow up to be big suckers. Large adult specimens of *Catostomus commersoni*, the common sucker, measure up to twenty-five inches in length. Sucker females are larger than the males.

In *The Tempest*, the jester Trinculo calls the savage Caliban a "deboshed [debauched] fish." Cotton Mather might have said the same of the sucker, an animal whose behavior, during an orgiastic week or two in springtime, would have left him mortified. But should we begrudge the sucker, as the Puritans might have, its greatest earthly pleasure? I think not. After all, perhaps the fish is simply receiving compensation for having to go through life, forever maligned, as a sucker.

4

The American Alligator

I n all the world, only two creatures can rightly call themselves alligators. One lives in China, the other in North America, and both are little changed from common ancestors that basked in Mesozoic swamps alongside the dinosaurs. To see an American alligator, you need only travel to the southeastern states where the big reptiles are abundant.

During a recent summer, my wife Debbie and I lived in Ocean Springs, Mississippi, where I had taken a temporary position as a naturalist with the National Park Service. I was based at Gulf Islands National Seashore, on Mississippi's Gulf Coast. To my delight, I found that seeing an alligator, in Ocean Springs and elsewhere along the coast, was as commonplace an event as glimpsing a white-tail deer in my native Northeast. In the park where I worked, for example, a small pond beside a road served as home to a seven-foot, one-eyed alligator we named Alphonse. During our early weeks in Mississippi, we visited Alphonse every day at lunchtime. We could usually find him sprawled across a mud bank, catching some sun, or lying low in the water with only his eyes and nostrils protruding above the surface. Although Alphonse never paid much attention to us, we enjoyed his company; when departing, I always derived particular satisfaction by saying, "See you later, alligator." (We often *did* see him later, because when I finished work several hours later, Alphonse was often sprawling or floating in the same place where we had left him.)

Sometimes people would feed Alphonse. This dangerous practice is illegal in Mississippi and punishable by a $500 fine; a sign reminding alligator watchers of this fact was mounted on a tree beside the pond. But it was not enough. Families in station wagons or groups of kids on bicycles would come with popcorn or marshmallows and throw them into the pond.

Alphonse, always on the lookout for a snack, would swim over, open his toothy mouth, and bite down on the tidbits, each snap of his jaws producing a dramatic splash. Aside from nutritional considerations, the danger of feeding an alligator in this way is that it will lose its natural shyness around humans and learn to associate extended arms and wiggling fingers with feeding. Then one day the alligator may grab a person—perhaps some-one who has no intention of feeding him—and drag him into the water. When this happens, the results may be fatal. Even if the human escapes with only a minor injury, the alligator is usu-ally branded "dangerous" and destroyed.

I like alligators (perhaps because of my fascination as a boy with dinosaurs) and rejoiced in the opportunity to live among them for a summer, but while in Mississippi, I must admit that at times their presence and abundance (an unseen presence for the most part) made me uncomfortable. One afternoon, for example, Debbie and I made a trip to the Pascagoula River marsh, a sort of compact, lesser known everglades in southeast Mississippi. We followed an old logging road into the woods, and there we found live oaks and cypresses teeming with song-birds—blue-gray gnatcatchers, hooded warblers, white-eyed vireos, and prothonotary warblers. Eventually we arrived at the edge of a swamp. It was a beautiful place, and I decided to shoot a self-timed photograph of the two of us with the swamp as a backdrop. As we stood waiting for the camera's shutter to click, I considered the scene behind us. A moment before, all had been peaceful. Cypress trunks rose out of the flat water like titanic pillars, and an unseen bird sang from a perch high in the canopy. Yet what if we were not alone? What if the swamp har-bored a large and very hungry alligator?

I tried to reassure myself. By virtue of their size and strength, alligators are potentially dangerous, but in all of recorded history there are few cases of unprovoked attacks upon humans. Yet I remained uneasy. Standing beside my bride at the edge of the southern swamp with our rear flank unprotected, I couldn't get the basic alligator facts and figures off my mind. Alligators can reach lengths of nineteen feet and more. They may weigh five hundred pounds. Adult male alligators bellow loudly when courting but approach a prospective meal silently and stealthily. Over a short distance, a healthy adult alligator can outrun a healthy adult human. Alligators often drown the animals they kill, then eat them whole.

With such thoughts swimming through my head, I waited somewhat nervously until the camera tripped. When it had, I spun around. The black, tannin-stained waters of the swamp were still calm. The prothonotary warblers still sang *zeet zeet zeet zeet* among the oaks and cypresses. No monster was in sight.

About a week later, as behind me a fat and swollen sun sank into the Gulf of Mexico, I stood by a pond listening to the singing of treefrogs. A ranger pulled up in his patrol car.

"Have you seen the alligator?" he said.

"What alligator?"

The ranger produced a big black flashlight of the sort that policemen carry and trained it on the pond. A few feet out, near a long dark log floating in the water, two objects spaced a few inches apart gave off a dull red glow.

"Gator eyes," said the ranger. I did not sleep well that night.

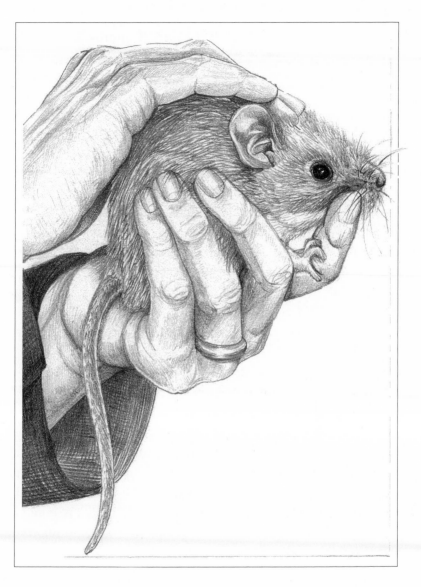

5
"Biofeelia"

One touch of nature makes the whole world kin. . . .
—*William Shakespeare,* Troilus and Cressida

Human beings, according to the eminent biologist Edward O. Wilson, possess an instinctive interest in the other living organisms with which they share the earth. Wilson labels this inborn human empathy for life *biophilia*. Biophilia, he says, is "the innate tendency to focus on life and lifelike processes."

I propose the coining of a similar term, of identical pronunciation, to describe a proclivity loosely connected to that described by Wilson. To wit: the human need to touch, or to contemplate the touching of, all natural objects. Let's call this powerful urge "biofeelia."

We *Homo sapiens* are a tactile species. Our sensitive fingertips and palms demand a steady diet of stimulation. Lucky for us, the world is full of interesting textures, consistencies, and irregularities. We are, therefore we touch. Our incessant compulsive tactile explorations of the world cease only when we die.

For literary naturalists, the tactile side of nature study has always been a touchy subject. When translated into writing, the sensations of fingers and palms tend to smack of the lurid— no matter how hard an author tries to make his accounts sound wholesome. Owing to some deeply entrenched quirk of human nature, words such as *touch* and *feel* come off sounding suggestive. Even the made-up word that serves as the title of this essay will probably raise a few eyebrows, and some readers may suspect that something racy will follow.

The urge to touch is powerful. Educational literature overflows with admonitions for teachers to provide children with opportunities to touch and feel. Little is said, however, of the

identical inclination in adults. I'm certain from my own observations that grown-ups like to touch things just as much as kids.

Over the years I've worked in three nature museums that
displayed taxidermic mounts of local wild animals. All three
places considered their stuffed specimens prized possessions,
and the people who worked with them did everything possible
to keep human fingers away from the fragile plumages and
pelages. Human hands inflict direct physical damage to taxidermic mounts; wherever they touch, hands leave behind oils
and acids that damage hair and fur. This is a serious problem for
curators because, just as dead men tell no lies, dead animals
grow no hair.

I found that no matter how forbidding the sign that says
"Hands Off!" and no matter how high or remote from people
the mounts are placed, stuffed animals in unprotected exhibits
are petted constantly and mercilessly. A handsome raccoon
mount, for example, has a shelf life little longer than a jar of
pickles. It will be touched, and touched again, until much hair
is lost. When the animal at last grows naked and repulsive, the
hands will seek satisfaction elsewhere.

One might think that most of the petting of museum
mounts is done by kids, but my observations suggest otherwise.
Parents are just as likely to run their fingers down the back of a
stuffed opossum as their children. In fact, they are more likely:
Mom and Dad enjoy a height advantage and longer reach than
Joanie and Junior. Putting mounts behind glass does not
entirely solve the problem. If animals cannot be touched, the
glass that shields them becomes a tactile substitute. In every
museum, removing fingerprints from exhibit cases is a never-
ending chore.

One cannot blame people for wanting to touch. Our urge
to explore inviting surfaces is more powerful than our logic. On

more than one occasion I have explained to a museum visitor that a mount should not be touched, and then watched in amazement as—while our conversation continued—the visitor's hand reached out unthinkingly to stroke the animal again. Everyone, it seems, is a "biofeeliac."

Speaking for myself, I cannot pass a friendly dog without stopping for a session of heavy petting. A wagging tail beckons to me like a siren. In crowded rooms dogs seek me out. They know instinctively, perhaps, that I'm a sucker for coats worn by their original owners.

Ever since I can remember, I've wanted to feel the pelage of a porcupine. Porcupines to my eyes are among the most cuddly and appealing of creatures, despite their barbs. But touching one presents obvious problems—even for a fellow porcupine. (One of the great wonders of the natural world is that porcupines somehow succeed in begetting offspring.) One spring afternoon, a woman walked into a nature museum where I was working and offered to donate a hand-raised porcupine. The porcupine was a female, about a year old, and friendly. The animal had outgrown her cage and was allowed the run of the house, but she was proving difficult to subdue at bedtime. And she was getting into mischief. Like all porcupines, this one chewed on wood, metal, and plastic. Anything she could sink her big pumpkin-colored incisors into she considered fair game.

I accepted the animal, named her Porky, and placed her in a large outdoor cage. From that moment on I was her keeper. The porcupine was leery of me at first. Whenever I appeared with food or came to clean her cage, she would vanish inside a crude den that I had fashioned for her out of lumber. In time, however, we reached an understanding and became devoted friends. I discovered that Porky loved to have her belly scratched. And she matched my finding with a simultaneous one of her own: that this human who provided her with food could be induced to tickle her underside. All that was required to get a scratching was for her to climb the wire of her cage, thus exposing her midriff, which was soft and lacked quills.

Touching living things can be pleasurable, but it also can have a practical side. Elm trees, for example, look much alike from one species to another but can be distinguished by running one's fingers over the upper surfaces of the leaves. American elm leaves feel leathery. They are thick and generally smooth. Slippery elm leaves, by contrast, are rough and their surfaces feel more like coarse sandpaper than cowhide. Why the name slippery elm? The slick part of the tree is not the leaf but the inner bark, which is pulpy and mucilaginous. The inner bark of the slippery elm has long been used in the manufacture of cough drops.

The sense of touch also comes in handy in identifying a woodland shrub called maple leaf viburnum. The leaves of this honeysuckle relative resemble the leaves of red and sugar maple trees. But the botanist who uses his fingers will never get the plants confused. Maple leaf viburnum leaves are soft and velvety while those of genuine maples are thin and smooth.

During the summer of 1980, while working for the National Park Service on the Florida coast, I learned that touch can also help to identify amphibians. One day in August, a naturalist friend, Mike Magley, and I clinched a salamander identification with incontrovertible evidence acquired by my fingertips. We had found a black, fairly large salamander that was unfamiliar to both of us. A quick scan of Roger Conant's *Field Guide to Reptiles and Amphibians* suggested that the animal was probably *Plethodon glutinosus*, a slimy salamander. But a slimy salamander had never been recorded in the park and we needed to be sure. Mike read down the list of field marks while I held the amphibian between my thumb and fingers.

"Length, four and three-quarters to six and three-quarters inches," said Mike.

"Yes."

"A large black salamander generally well sprinkled with silvery-white flecks."

"Check."

"Under surfaces normally plain slate color; chin and throat, although somewhat lighter, are definitely dark."

"Yes, clearly."

"Skin-gland secretions cling to your hands like glue and almost have to wear off."

"Oh my god." Conant was right. The stuff was all over my fingers, clinging to the skin like epoxy. Mike fell over laughing. The park had a new salamander for its list. And the slime clung to my fingers for a week, defying all attempts at scrubbing it off.

To touch or not to touch: there really isn't any question.